As a former MK (Missionary Kid) ... mother, Christy Brawner offers a r ... at her personal faith. With remark ... ences with such diverse subjects as loneliness, eating, dating, marriage, and childbirth and the spiritual lessons she learned through successfully facing each of them. This book sparkles with Christy's vibrant personality. It testifies of Christ's sufficiency in all of life's circumstances and gives insights into how a modern young woman can be both real and spiritual simultaneously.

> —Robin Hadaway, Associate Professor of Missions
> Midwestern Baptist Theological Seminary

Christy Akins Brawner writes with a transparency that is refreshing and inspirational. For a generation in search of purpose, she offers real stories about real relationships—and her own story is complete with the powerful love of Jesus Christ. Christy is a woman of vision, integrity, and service.

> —Andrew Westmoreland, President
> Ouachita Baptist University

I've known Christy Akins Brawner for more than a dozen years. I've watched God bless her life and ministry. I'm not at all surprised she's written this book. She speaks with passion and authority—with honesty about her own struggles and how God has seen her through them. Like a trusted friend, she offers in this book to take readers by the hand and to gently say, "Here's the way. Follow me." My prayer is that those who read this book *will* hear and heed Christy's wise and loving counsel.

> —B. Dale Ellenburg, Academic Vice-President
> Mid-America Baptist Theological Seminary

Christy Brawner takes the reader through universal problems and fears people have while they grow into maturity. She is clear, frank, and transparent about her struggles. As Christy applies solid biblical truths in the crucible of the cultural wars in which we live, this book especially will appeal to 20-somethings as they shape their perspectives on life.

> —Avery T. Willis Jr., Emeritus Senior Vice President
> International Mission Board, SBC

Christy Brawner's story rekindles the fires of our hearts to know, love, and walk with the Living God. Her honesty about her struggles, her confessions of failure as well as her testimonies of success, and her willingness to share what she's gone through make this book both a joy and a challenge to read. Joy occurs as she shares her heart and we see God's work; challenge occurs when she calls us to live out this same walk with God. I commend this book to every person wanting honesty and intimacy with Jesus the Lord.

—Stan May, Professor and Chairman, Department of Missions
Mid-America Baptist Theological Seminary

HOW TO BE
SPIRITUAL
WITHOUT BEING
WEIRD

12 CORE VALUES FOR THRIVING
IN A MODERN WORLD

CHRISTY BRAWNER

HANNIBAL BOOKS
www.hannibalbooks.com

Printed in the United States of America
by Versa Press, East Peoria, IL
Cover design by Greg Crull
Scripture taken from the Holy Bible, *New International Version*,
copyright 1973, 1978, 1984 by International Bible Society
Library of Congress Control Number: 20059936531
ISBN 0-929292-35-9

Hannibal Books
P.O. Box 461592
Garland, Texas 75046
1-800-747-0738
www.hannibalbooks.com

Dedication

Dearest Anna Katherine and Elizabeth,

I wrote this book for you. I have so much I want to share with you—so many mistakes I want you to avoid and so much of life I want you to experience. Being your guardians is the most precious gift and awesome responsibility our Almighty God ever gave your father and myself. We love you with all our hearts and souls and pray daily that God will protect and guide you all the days of your life.

May you always remember that God has given you the greatest of all gifts: LIFE. I never will forget the days you were born, but you always must remember that you were created for eternity. You were created to abide in His love and thrive in His victory.

With your blessed future in mind, I dedicate this book to you.

Your mother,

Christy

Contents

Foreword

Christy Brawner is a thriver in the modern world. By trusting God for the present and the future, she thrived in the midst of cross-cultural living—especially through struggles and tragedies such as the death of her mom on the mission field.

Christy not only talks the talk but truly walks the walk. I know, because I am her dad. From the time she gave her life to Christ until now, she has shared the gospel one-on-one—both in the streets and in small groups. She connects with this generation like no one I know.

Early on I discovered in Christy an extraordinary and remarkable ability to go deep into God's Word and to draw highly accurate applications to daily life. This is what she has done in this book. She speaks in the vernacular of her generation.

Christy relates exceptionally well not only to Christians but also to non-believing young people even though she was, as she states, brought up in a Christian home and learned the Word of God around our family table and in church. She relates well to people who don't have a clue, even though she was reared in the exact opposite circumstances—on the international mission field involved in the lives of non-believers and winning them to Christ.

This book is about how to thrive in a modern world. By learning and applying these 12 basic, fundamental principles of life, you, too, will be a "thriver."

The Bible is a book full of God's principles of life. If we understand them and obey them, this will lead to peace, joy, and fulfillment. If we choose not to obey them, this path will lead to destruction in various areas of our lives. Many people suffer the consequences because they do not even know the principles. In a unique story-telling style Christy captures the attention of the reader as she explains each of these 12 basic principles. The reader not only will be able to understand the principles but also learn to apply them.

I trust God will use this book to help you become a person who "thrives" for the glory of Jesus Christ.

Wade Akins, Career Missionary
International Mission Board, SBC

Preface

As I sat at a monitor in the crowded Internet cafe, the sandy brown-haired man next to me turned, smiled, and asked to borrow a pen. I glanced at his screen and saw that, over the Internet, he was "going out" with a very cute young woman. After signing off with her, he began to chat with me. He recently was divorced. After 12 years of marriage and a beautiful daughter, his wife had to "move on." He told me that he chatted on the Internet while he waited for his daughter to get out of school. "I lost my wife, all of our friends, and my entire life. All I have is my precious daughter. I've got to start over somehow," he confided.

After finishing this conversation, I glanced over at the long eyelashed, 20-something brunette using the computer on my right. On her screen was an application to join an Internet dating site. This sparked my curiosity; I gazed down the row at all the people using computers. To my amazement I was the only one NOT Internet dating! No one was talking. No one was studying. Everyone was looking for a friend.

We all seem to be lonely. We have no shortage of entertainment, stress, loud music, and stuff to do, but in the midst of it all, we are bored and alone. We have no one to trust. We have no one to love. We don't even have anyone to feed our pets when we're on vacation! Self-promotion to try to find others lonely like us is the only game in town.

Is this how God planned for the world to become?

The answer is a most emphatic "NO!" The Bible teaches that we were created for love. We were created for relationships. We were created for a "living hope"! But, if this is true, how can we live in such a way that we experience life the way God designed? How do we find love, joy, excitement, and fulfillment—the kinds that last forever?

The pages of this book search the answer to this question. They outline 12 core values that every person must embrace and live out, IF he or she wants to live and thrive in this world as we fulfill the purpose our Creator designed for survival. In a way that is both humorous and understandable, we will look at how God views those things that are important to us: love, intimacy, dating, money, fear, and friendship. We will look at what is involved in being spiritual without becoming strangely "religious" or "weird." We will look at how God, in the sacred Scriptures of the Bible, addresses these key issues. We will see how, if we obey God in the practical areas, He will fill our lives with the excitement and adventure that He designed for us to experience.

Value 1

Finding the Essence of Love

Five minutes after we walked onto our little international-school campus in Belo Horizonte, Brazil, Becky and I became best friends. We connected at the soul and shared a common restlessness of spirit. We competed for the lead in plays, scaled mountains, and, explored the urban "jungle" that defines modern Brazil. Neither of us had a "pause" button. Life was a whirlwind; we couldn't stop spinning. However, being teen-age girls is competitive—even if you live in Latin America and even if your parents are missionaries.

Both of us were cute, smart, musical, and athletic enough for a high school of our embarrassingly small size. We were, as were all the other students, involved in every aspect of school life—both social and academic. However, I had an Achilles heel. Between the two of us I was more bookish; Becky was all glamour. If one were to describe it in Scooby-Doo terms, I was Velma and she, Daphne. We were competitive in every other area, but when the subject of boys was involved, I was destined for second place. Everywhere we went, to my dismay, boys fell at her feet in adoration. Her attraction seemed magical. She received long declarations of undying love from boys she hardly knew. Older guys would leave her presence and rush home to make sentimental videos and gushy poems. She got presents in the mail and desperate phone calls in the middle of the night. Becky was the first real-life Siren I ever had met.

Fortunately Becky didn't take herself too seriously. We always had a good laugh at the latest of what eventually became a long list of desperate, love-stricken pups. Always on the sidelines and never on the field, I became a student of love's mesmerizing effects on people. These boys would use the "L" word; the power of it would drive them to actions beyond their control. In fact, to be in love with someone, as I observed, was, in fact to be "out of control." It involved letting someone else control you, possess your thoughts, and drive your actions. As the "Logical Velma", I found love to be illogical and difficult to understand but undeniably powerful. It seemed to be a source of courage—an identity. Although I never told Becky, I, too, longed to be a part of the madness.

God, the Almighty Creator of the universe, was the one who invented the bemusing concept we call love. He created it and put the pursuit of true love deep inside the heart of every breathing human being. We feel it the moment we are born and immediately crave it. However, as most of us grow up, love, like money, seems all too elusive. Men and women, young and old, hope to feel love from others. Yet often hope turns to despair. We realize that love never seems to be freely given.

In response to this hopelessness God became a human being and Christ was sent to earth. He spent His entire ministry explaining to us what love means. Love was the principal reason He was on earth. First and foremost we find love through a personal relationship with God Himself.

At age 15 I found love completely elusive and difficult to define. But the Bible defines its essence: God IS love. Since then, 17 years, one husband and two children later, I still only am beginning to understand the depth of this superhuman experience. However, three things I know for sure. It is real. It is supernatural; and it is within reach.

You shall love the Lord your God with all your heart, with all your soul, with all your mind, and with all your strength (1 Sam. 16:7).

This is the first of the Ten Commandments. When the religious Hebrews asked Jesus what he considered to be the most important commandment of all, this was His answer.

I was reared in a very religious home. At night while she tucked me in, my mother sang lullabies of God's love. The first sentence I ever spoke actually was "Jesus Loves Me." From my very crib I was instructed that "God is love. I love God."

But such a simplistic assertion begs a complex question: How can anyone really love God? What does loving God mean? He is not here to hug or touch. He cannot be seen. How can He be experienced? Yet, Jesus did not merely say, "Love God." He said, "Love God with ALL your heart, with ALL your soul, with ALL your mind, and with ALL your strength." He repeated "All" four times and reemphasized every part of our being. God wants us to be driven passionately through life with the power that springs an all-consuming love. But, to love God in the way we're commanded—with our ALL— how can we realistically do this? Does it really make a difference?

To know who to love first and foremost is to have direction. It is to have meaning—to know your future. If we truly can love God with every ounce of our existence, our lives then will be played out according to His purpose. Our lives were meant to be lived this way. Feeling completely loved is to have a life filled with meaning. We never were made to struggle with crises of underconfidence and loneliness. We were not created to live in a world of eternal dissatisfaction. God's design is that we know and understand our value in God and that we live abundantly in His peace. We were made to live a life fueled and filled with love created by a deep and personal relationship with Him.

But HOW?

It starts in the heart!!

When Christ addresses the most critical issue of human existence, He starts with the heart. This is not by accident. This would seem like an obvious choice if He were talking to teen-aged girls. But, in fact, at the moment the question is posed, He is staring into the faces of grave, old, deathly serious civil and political figures who were decked out in intentionally intimidating religious uniforms. He says, "Love the Lord your God with all of your heart, soul, and strength." In other words, He's saying, "Filter every emotion, every fledgling sense of passion, anger, or excitement through your devotion to Me. Recognize and live in the understanding that I, Jesus Christ, am THE primary relationship in your life to which all else must be subject: every relationship, every activity, every desire, and aspiration. Love Me unrestrained and in total trust."

His listeners rejected His advice. It was unacceptable.

Even now His message remains unacceptable. To live today in a manner acceptable to Christ is to pay a high price. It means putting into play personal cash, opportunity for advancement, and fun. Ultimately, it involves a surrender of the most basic rights of being human: the right to control one's own destiny. Is it worth doing so?

When my daughter, Elizabeth, turned 4, she suddenly "found religion." It became an instant device in all of her arguments. I remember one specific day when she and her sister were playing in McDonald's playland. Her daddy called out to her, "Elizabeth, wash your hands. Your food is here." She sassily replied, "Why? You're not the boss." He instructed her, "Lizzy, I AM your boss", to which she quickly replied, "No, God's the boss." A family friend asked her who was the oldest person in our family. She said, "God. He's infinity." Once, her sister, Anna, demanded a toy. Anna said, "Gimme that. I'm bigger." Elizabeth flatly refused. She asserted, "No, God's the most biggest." For her, God is her ace. Even though she's the smallest, she's got an ally. He's the most of everything. Even at 4 her mind is sophisticated enough to know that an all-powerful God is out there—a God Who's the Most of everything!

The existence of God simply is the only logical explanation to the powerful yet fragile nature of the universe, the human body, and our own existence. It's obvious. In fact, finding someone that dares to challenge God in this way is difficult. This is not the problem. But to know an all-powerful Being exists who is in charge of the universe is a far cry from falling in love with Him. It's actually quite the opposite.

To see God in the radiance of His power is to stand in the face of fear. In the last book of the Bible the Apostle John saw Jesus in the "awesome radiance of His Power." The Bible said John looked at Him and then fell at His feet as dead. John was in a state of total fear. He was not alone: Moses, Isaiah, and Ezekiel did the same thing. In fact anyone who ever has been recorded as having a metaphysical experience with the Most High God walked away in a state of horrific awe. He, in His pure visible glory as Judge and Ruler, is no comfort to a wavering heart. God is the Most High King. A Being on a high throne surrounded by giant angels with monstrous wings is no teddy bear or emotional crutch. His power is fearfully overwhelming.

14

Love, however, is the opposite. Love defies fear. It is personal. Love is nearness. Love is NOT philosophical. It is not even "religious." It is felt through the experience of living. It grows through relationship, time, and distress. It also is unique. Every love relationship in the world has its own special meaning and is shaped in its own distinctive way.

The great mystery encompassing God is not His power and genius; those things are undeniably self-evident. It is His desire to have a relationship with each human being that baffles us. It is His passion for the individual. The Bible says that God knows and actually cares how many strands of hair are on the head of every person ever born. Matthew included in his gospel that the Almighty God even is interested in things as temporal as flowers and birds.

But what is more interesting than the fact that God cares for nature is to realize that God is capable of loving each person in the world more than any one of us ever could love each other. He desires for every one of us to know Him in an intimate way and to learn to love as He loves us. Not only do the expanses of the universe make God awe inspiring, HIS capacity for unconditional love for the individual should bend the knee even of the strongest agnostic. The expanse of one is equal to the expanse of the other.

On an airplane I sat next to a man from England. We both were on our way to Las Vegas. After he learned my profession, he started to tell me his thoughts on God. He began with His view of God's love. He said, "I just don't believe that God gives a d---. I cannot believe that a God as big as the universe could even care." He could picture God as a Creator. But God as an intimate friend? Never.

I graduated from high school with a French boy named Benoit. He was a wonderful person with a great sense of humor and even bigger heart. Every day we'd hang out in the student lounge during lunch. However, the more I got to know Benoit, the more I could not possibly overlook the sadness in his eyes, even when he was laughing. At age 18 he already lived his life in a way that expressed a total sense of hopelessness. He drank every day: things like vodka, whiskey, and bourbon. All day long he smoked cigarettes— sometimes two or three simultaneously. Most days he continually slipped in quick smokes in the school bathroom between classes or behind the gym. He was intellectually bright, but the things Benoit did to his body were totally destructive. I heard several of our classmates pull him over after some reckless episode and say, "Benoit, cool it with the liquor. You're too young to die." But Benoit always answered them the same way: "If you die, you're dead. So what?" He said this so often, it became something of a coined phrase. One day, I found on the bulletin board by the library a sign Benoit had left on poster board. The sign read, "If you die, you're dead. So what?"

What was missing from Benoit's life? The same God that created me had created Benoit. God knew all the hairs of his head, as He knew mine. God created Benoit with a special purpose for his life, just as I knew that He had me. Yet, if this were all true, then why was his life filled with despair and mine with joy and hope? This can't be fair. I suppose one could psychoanalyze my friend and blame a host of circumstances for his sadness. But really, the answer is very simple and likewise universal: Benoit did not experience God's love; I did. God always has loved Benoit every bit as much as he loves me. But Benoit did not know how to feel it. What's even worse, Benoit did not love Him in return.

Benoit taught me what being alive and not really living meant. His life had no meaning. He was existing and breathing because of the grace of God, but his soul was hollow. His heart was empty. He felt this but could not understand it. This resulted in despair.

We never were created to be alone. We were created for intimacy. We were created for companionship. We were created for a love relationship that starts with the Creator of the Universe. His love brings us into this world. He gives us life because He loves us. He gives us breath because He wants us to spend our days here learning to know and love Him.

"You shall love the Lord your God with ALL your heart; with ALL your soul, with ALL your mind, and with ALL your strength" (Mark 12:30). Live in a deep and meaningful love relationship with Him. In this book I hope to share how to experience such a life. Doing this is possible, despite any odds that are against you, how much you already have messed up, or whatever cards life has dealt you.

I hope to share with you a hope through the experiences of my life, not because my life is remarkable. It isn't. But my hope is that by my tracing God's faithfulness to me, you will see His faithfulness to you. His faithfulness is universal, but every story is unique.

* * * * * * * * *

In April 1971 Wade Akins stood in the living room of his future in-laws and married Sherry Deakins, a young woman from Gray, TN. Both Wade and Sherry loved God with all their hearts. They vowed to love God and honor Him in their marriage. Eighteen months later, I was born: Christy Renee Akins. We lived in Washington, DC. Daddy had what people called a "faith ministry." My mother and he worked with street people and students. We lived off contributions. Since neither street people nor students are known for their wealth, cash was a problem in those days, but that didn't stress me out. We were all very happy. I was happy.

I loved my family. I loved my God. I loved my life. I easily could believe that God loved me. He had given me everything; that was the way life always was going to be. One day my mother explained God's loving sacrifice through the birth and death of Jesus Christ. She told me that Christ was sent to earth to pay the price for my sin. If I would ask Him to enter my heart, He would forgive me for anything wrong I ever would do. He would be with me forever. One day, alone in my room, I very simply and undramatically asked God to forgive me for my sins and enter my heart. I was young, but I was serious. I had seen others do it. I wanted to give my heart, soul, mind and body to Jesus Christ, just as my mother and father had. To this day, I find this difficult to believe. How could God even take me seriously? I was too little. How did I even know what I was doing? But, I trusted Him. I knew He was real. I could feel Him. I knew He always would take care of me. It was an easy step of faith. Of course, God would do what's best for me. That was all I knew. I could feel His presence everywhere. I never had doubt.

When I was 10 years old, my parents decided to sell our home in Washington and become Baptist missionaries to Brazil. That sounded exciting. How cool would learning another language be? I was guaranteed to see monkeys. I was especially excited about riding on a real airplane. I couldn't believe how good God was to us. After a rough start adjusting to a new world and language, I was not disappointed. Brazil is a wonderful country; I learned to love it.

At age 17 I graduated from the "Escola Americana de Belo Horizonte." Things had gone well for me. God had been good. But now, for the first time in my life, things were changing. This time I was being forced to leave my home, my friends, and my family. The time had arrived for college. Except for me, college meant 5,000 miles away from everything with which I was familiar and which I loved. In my head, I knew college was an awesome privilege not shared by many in the world, but my heart hurt when I held the roses and through the tiny airplane window waved goodbye.

After one semester of school, the time arrived to say goodbye again. This time, I took my mother, father, and two brothers to the airport. They had returned to the U.S. with me, now the time arrived for them to get on an airplane and fly home to Brazil without me. From now on, I was to be all by myself in America.

I never will forget going to the airport that day. I felt a knife plunging into my chest as I hugged their necks one by one. My eyes filled with tears. I could hardly speak. I stood in the parking lot and watched their plane take off. Long after the plane was gone from view, I stared into the empty clouds.

I felt alone! I turned around and walked to the car. I actually wasn't alone. My grandmother was with me and drove me back to her house, but I didn't even acknowledge her presence. My chest and throat filled with painful tears. I hurt so much to let them go. This wasn't fair. Why would God do this to me? I didn't deserve it!

I embraced the pain of their absence as I made the drive back to school. I didn't listen to the radio or put in any tapes. I was quiet. I let the tears fall down my cheeks. However, in the silence, I felt God's presence in a way I never had felt it before. It was the presence of peace. It was like feeling at home near my mother, but yet, I wasn't. That day something special happened to me. God renewed my spirit during the 3 1/2 hours on the windy back roads of Louisiana and Arkansas. I learned that the Almighty God of the universe is enough. His love could be alive in my life and produce a joy and energy independent of life's circumstances. I still was sad. I still missed my family in an overwhelming way, but I did not feel alone. I did not despair.

I didn't have any planned spiritual encounter that day. I didn't listen to Christian radio or stop to read any Bible passages. It was just real; I felt it. God spoke to my heart. He said, "I'm here. I always will be here. You never will be alone." That day I learned that a person who has given his or her heart to Christ cannot be isolated from God's presence. Many years earlier I had entered into a love covenant with Jesus Christ, but I still was to learn that His love can sustain.

Two-and-a-half years later, as a junior in college, I chose to become an exchange student to the newly independent country of Kazakhstan. For more than 50 years Kazakhstan had been a part of the Soviet Union. The infrastructure of the country was large, militaristic, technologically deficient, and practically dysfunctional for the everyday resident. We stood in lines for bread, lines for meat, and lines for butter. One day, in a moment of sheer luck, our little exchange group bought six cases of cooking oil on the black market. It was unavailable anywhere in town. On the local economy we paid a small fortune for this luxury. Native people long since had learned to cook with the fat trimmed from their meat. One month later, our apartment was burglarized. The only things the thieves took were a bottle of vanilla extract and our cases of cooking oil. They even left the cash.

Communication in Alma-Ata (as the capital was called at that time) was erratic and random. Mail always arrived late and opened. Sometimes it would not arrive at all. Telephones were rare; telephone lines were problematic. To talk on the telephone we would have to find a private resident who did not object to our using his or her phone for a very expensive international phone call. Then we would place a call to the operator and ask her to make the international connection for us. In every instance she would tell us to stand by as she tried to place the call. We would sit by the phone and wait for up to eight hours for the phone to ring and the operator to inform us that our call had been patched through. Over the course of my stay in Alma-Ata, information with the outside world became more and more scarce. I felt increasingly more isolated.

One day, however, a school official told me that I had received a fax. No one in our exchange group ever had received a fax before, even though we had known that one did, in fact, exist in the city. Our families had been given the number. The fax machine was situated in a government ministry. It was a rare day indeed. I felt excitement. Everyone else felt envy.

After class I pulled out my directions to the ministry and eagerly took a crowded tram downtown to pick up my fax. I was eager to receive word from my family members. The most recent letter I had received from them had been mailed more than a month before. I can remember smiling from ear to ear as the official handed me my paper. *Blagadayubas*, I said. This roughly translates into "thank you, thank you, thank you, thank you very, very much." I turned and hurried out into the street to find an empty park bench. I was excited to read the news from home.

The letter began with my mother's usual, cheerful chit-chat about my brothers' activities and my old friends. It was just the kind of thing I had been hoping to receive. However, after the first few paragraphs the tone of the letter changed completely. I began to understand the reason for the fax. My mother had been diagnosed with a terminal disease. It already had debilitated her lungs to 50 percent of their normal capacity. It was attacking her intestines and other vital organs. She had no way to know how long she would live. She was hopeful, but the doctors were sure that a definite countdown of her days had begun.

I felt as though someone had taken a rock and had thrown it against my head. I reread her prognosis and sat stunned. I could not have been farther away geographically from her; she was going to die. I stared into an old, empty drain in the road and really didn't even think. My mind swirled in a blur.

The next year, three weeks before Christmas, I received the dreaded phone call. My mother unexpectedly had died in our home in Brazil. The last time I had seen her was for a brief visit that summer after I returned from Russia.

The pain of such news initially is very shocking. I had been at a sorority event in Memphis when my roommate received the phone call. My boyfriend drove me back to our college town, where my brother waited for me at a professor's home. When I saw my brother, the tears poured out. I cried. He cried. The pain was overwhelming. I couldn't believe it.

That night I remember going to my bedroom and staring at my Bible. I didn't know what to think. Why would God do this? Nothing justified this. My mother was a faithful and selfless servant of the Lord. No one could have been more totally undeserving of a premature death. I tried to open my Bible and read it, but I couldn't force my eyes to focus on the page. I opened my prayer journal, but I couldn't write. Where was my God?

I closed my notebook and stared at the painted cinderblocks of my dorm room wall. Just because my Bible was still in my lap, I aimlessly picked it up again. I skeptically brushed through the pages and thought, *What could God say to me now?* Then I randomly opened the Word of God smack dab in the middle. I stared at a bunch of psalms. Up to this point in my life I never really had enjoyed or understood many of the psalms. I had always found them too poetic and redundant. But this evening my eyes fell on the pages. Words of God through David, his servant, penetrated my heart: "Precious in the sight of the Lord is the death of His saints. O Lord, truly I am Your servant; I am Your servant, the son of Your maidservant; You have loosed my bonds. I will offer to You the Sacrifice of thanksgiving, And will call upon the name of the Lord" (Ps. 116:15-17).

The Lord spoke to me again that day. As I read the same passage over and over again, I felt His gracious hand bring peace to my heart. He said to me, "Christy, neither you nor your mother is being punished. I love you as I love your mother. You are subject to the evils of the world into which you were born, but they will NOT overcome you. Remember, you never will be alone. I am with you. I have overcome the evil of your world. For this you can give thanks."

During the next several months, I reread this same passage of Scripture hundreds and hundreds of times as I dealt with the loss of my mother. I remembered vividly the message the Lord had delivered to me that night. During the dark days of grief I hung on His promise. Many nights I would drive in my car into the backwoods of Arkansas just to cry. I was embarrassed to be seen like that on campus. My heart was broken; the pain was intense. But I was not alone. I knew the Lord loved me.

How does a person survive when knocked down by death, disease, heartbreak, and pain? Only through a true, love relationship with God Almighty. He not only is the Creator and Sustainer of the Universe, He also is the Creator and Sustainer of our souls.

He loves us and desires to express His love to us in incomprehensible ways. He desires to comfort us and shelter us against the violent winds of a fallen world. Yet this relationship does not hinge on His desire alone. He has given us free will. Only of our own free will do we submit to the authority and protection of His wings. We must choose to love Him. The Bible says, "Eye has not seen, nor ear heard, Nor have entered into the heart of man the things which God has prepared for those who love Him" (1 Cor. 2:9).

My experience has been that God's love is enough. Today I sit in a home filled with more material possessions than I can enumerate. I have an amazing husband who loves me, two beautiful daughters, a college degree, and a graduate degree I couldn't afford. These are examples of big things. But God is not just about big things. He has thrown me parties, taken me around the world, brought friends into my life, kept money in the bank, and helped me regain flat abs! He has been there from the time I was a little girl until today. I can testify before the highest court in any land that God's love lasts a lifetime. It envelops us when we feel attacked. It challenges us when we need to be pushed. It lifts us up when we need to see over obstacles. Jesus Christ ALWAYS is enough.

I can honestly say that Becky and I had a silly concept of love. We obviously had no idea what true love was all about. We still

22

don't. God is unraveling this mystery before each of us a day at a time. God always has loved us. Falling in love with Him is safe. He has planned a life full of surprises. His love is everlasting and sustainable. It teaches us how to live our lives in a way that honors Him.

My desire for you is that you may learn to live your life worthy of the God who created you. I pray that you may accept the challenge to love God in the way He created you to do so—that you will fulfill the purpose of your life and live it with dignity and honor. It is a journey of a lifetime, but once we start, we cannot turn back. The beginning is the pursuit of intimacy. Let's learn how!

Value 2

Unveiling Intimacy

I could not relate to having a baby. I never had babysat. I had no nieces or nephews. None of my friends ever had had a baby. I never even had volunteered to keep the nursery at church. The closest I ever was to babies was occasionally sitting near them on airplanes and listening to them scream when the air pressure made their teeny ears pop during takeoff. My husband, Jeff, and I knew we were having a baby. We knew she was arriving. In our heads we knew that meant change, but beyond that, everything was a blur until September 24, 1998.

Anna Katherine had been given her name just a few days after we learned she was a girl. We had read the parenting books, attended all the childbirth classes, and learned infant CPR. Before she ever had taken her first real breath, in our own minds, we were accomplished parents. However, until 1 a.m., on September 24, we really had only a shadow knowledge of who Anna Katherine was—a fuzzy, black-and-white ultrasound image with words pointing to her identifiable body parts. We knew all about her, how she was being created, what she was going to do when she was born, what she would need, what she would eat. But the truth was, until Dr. Opie lifted her up and Jeff cut the umbilical cord, we had no idea who she really was.

On the evening of September 22, 1998, two-and-a-half weeks past the original due date, Dr. Opie called and said, "Do you want to have this baby tomorrow? Be at the hospital at 5 a.m." We were so excited. We went to the video store and rented *The Giant* to watch in the recovery room, packed our clothes, put the car seat into our car, and picked out our favorite junk food to put in the recovery-room refrigerator. Sleeping through the night was impossible. We were up and out the door before 4:30 the next morning. This was going to be so fun!

Obviously, we never were going to get around to our junk food and video. The process was slow. The labor was induced, so I began receiving meds through an IV. At first the contractions were sporadic and not really painful. By 11 a.m. I had been in labor for five-and-a-half hours. I felt great and was experiencing only minor discomfort. Dr. Opie visited me. I still was giggly with excitement. Foolishly I believed myself to be Wonder Woman. In order to speed things up, I agreed to accept an epidural only much later in the labor process. Dr. Opie went to his office for the day and left written instructions with the nurse.

Not long after the doctor left, I began to experience the real pain. I hurt really badly. I hurt so badly that I called in the nurse to request pain medication. "NO," she replied. "Your labor is taking too long. You are not to get your epidural until you are farther along. You discussed this with your doctor. I have written instructions to wait. Any medication now will slow down the process."

UGH! What had I been thinking? The pain intensified. By 1 p.m., I thought I was on the verge of passing out. I called the nurse in again. This time I begged her the way I had seen beggars do on the street corners of Brazil. She remained firm in her position. I felt hopeless. Just as she checked my IV next to my bed, a contraction again rolled over me. I chose to resort to violence. Grabbing her as though I were giving her a bear hug, I pounded her on the back. "Please, please, PLEASE, bring in the doctor," I begged as I hit her.

Although the nurse liked me a lot less after her beating, she did agree to call Dr. Opie. By 2:30 that afternoon, I once again was a pleasant, smiling person—blissfully living through the graces of modern medicine. With the shift change, I even had a second shot at making a good impression on a delivery nurse.

But Anna Katherine still would not emerge. By 10 that night my family and friends had waited the entire day. Everyone, myself included, began to get concerned. Dr. Opie broke my water and forced my body into intense labor. For two-and-a-half more hours I pushed with all the strength I could muster, but still no baby.

I began to have fever; the baby showed signs of significant stress. I remember seeing Dr. Opie call Jeff to go over into a corner.

Both of them arrived to tell me that emergency surgery was necessary.

I was wheeled passed an entourage of all my friends and family in the hallway on my way to the OR. I could hear words of encouragement and cheers. Everything was going to be all right. The OR was cold; the lights were very bright. My epidural was increased. I felt nothing below my waist. Jeff had the camera and was wearing green scrubs. I heard clicking and clanking of instruments. I could smell the singe of burnt flesh. Dr. Opie was leading the operating team. His voice was calm. He was telling Jeff all the names of my inner organs—gross! No one seemed anxious. But this was taking a long time. I was beginning to get sleepy. Finally I heard the scream of little Anna Katherine. They showed her to me and told me she was scoring high on the Apgar scale. Then they told me that she had a fever and must immediately go the ICU. I was not to worry, but I would not be able to hold her until her fever subsided. It was OK, Jeff said. He was going to the ICU, too. I would have to go to my room and wait for Anna Katherine's body to fight the infection. Everything was hazy. Everyone was talking fast. I was thirsty and tired. I allowed myself to be overcome with exhaustion and fell into a deep sleep.

Four hours later Jeff walked into my room and woke me up. "I have someone I want you to meet," he said, "Say hello to Anna Katherine Brawner." WOW! It really had happened!

I still remember looking at the baby and being overwhelmed with the most powerful emotion I ever had felt in my entire life. It covered my whole body like a heavy blanket. I had goosebumps. I was overpowered instantly with the intensity of a love different than I ever had felt before. The object of my love was this beautiful 24-inch, 8-pound 10-ounce, blue-eyed, black-haired baby. I looked at Jeff, who had a crooked smile and teary eyes and knew that he felt it, too.

But that first moment was to be only the beginning. I took her home and realized I was being introduced to something that I never had experienced before. I was connected to this baby in a way that was completely unique. She depended on me for life itself. I loved

26

her even more for it. I was filled with fear. What if something happens to her? What if I don't feed her properly? What if she gets sick? What if she stops breathing? The first night she was home, I could not bear to put her in the nursery we so lovingly had decorated in the next room of our apartment. What if someone sneaked in our apartment and grabbed her?

We pulled a cradle next to our bed; I laid her there. I was panic-stricken and couldn't sleep for the first few nights. I sat up every few minutes and stared at her. I continually checked to see if she still were breathing. I looked at her and thought, "How could a person possibly love another person as much as we love you? This is impossible. If we ever lost you, our lives would become meaningless immediately." I remember thinking how odd I felt feeling that way about someone I had known less than a day. But at the moment I knew it was real.

I since have learned that those emotions that I experienced those first days, however true, were just the beginning. Today, as I write this, Anna Katherine is much older. And today, I can say that the love I felt for her that day only was the beginning. Jeff and I love both of our daughters, Anna Katherine and Elizabeth, more deeply now than we ever did when they were born. Our love for them only has grown with age. Probably more than one reason exists for this, but the main and most obvious reason is that we know them better now. I know what Anna likes and dislikes. I know what seeing her smile and laugh is like. I know how I felt while carrying her limp body to the hospital in fear. I remember the day she learned to ride a bike and swim across the pool. I have watched her ballet recitals and helped her learn notes on the piano. I have seen her cry at disappointment and rejoice in success. And I also know that in 10 years I will not love her less but love her more.

The reason I have taken the time to describe this relationship this way is because God has chosen to identify Himself first and foremost to us as God the Father. In the Lord's Prayer we are to pray, "Our Father." He wants me to approach Him as Father—not God, our Father—just Our Father. To me this association highlights the two most important features of our relationship with Him: first

His love for us, which we discussed in the last chapter, and second the intimacy He desires to share with us.

One of the many bizarre encounters that Jesus had with people seeking to understand Him occurred with a man named Nicodemus. The Bible describes Nicodemus as a "ruler of the Jews." He, for whatever reason, approached Jesus in the middle of the night to ask Him who He was. Jesus answered Nicodemus with an analogy, albeit less lengthy, like the story I just described. He said, "Unless one is born again, he cannot see the kingdom of God (John 3:2)."

Nicodemus tried to point out to Jesus the ridiculous nature of this statement, "How can a man be born when he is old? Can he enter a second time into his mother's womb and be born?"

Jesus answered, "Most assuredly, I say to you, unless one is born of water and the Spirit, he cannot enter the kingdom of God. That which is born of the flesh is flesh, and that which is born of the Spirit is spirit. Do not marvel that I said to you. You must be born again."

Christ loves everyone. This has been so from the beginning of time. The Bible says that He breathes into each person the breath of life. This itself is an act of love. We are born the first time by the will of God. He doesn't ask our permission. He doesn't seek the permission of our parents. He just does it. However, this is only half of the story. To have intimacy with God, to have the kind of complete existence that He has prepared for us, we must "be born again." This is something that God does NOT force on us. He asks us to enter voluntarily into a relationship with him.

The Bible says that we are born as sinners; we naturally do things that displease God. We lie, steal, harbor anger and jealousy, hurt others, and on the list goes. These kinds of things are contrary to God's nature. He cannot coexist or be a part of anything so flawed. This was the reason that Christ died on the cross. The story is more complex, but the Bible teaches that Christ died to be able to forgive us our sins. He paid the penalty for sin, so that we may be restored to a right relationship with God.

When we accept the terms of this relationship, we are "born again." What this means is that each person admits in his or her heart that he or she has sinned. We admit that this sin is something that is wrong and deserves the death penalty before God. We then ask God to forgive our sin through the blood sacrifice of Jesus Christ. We then GIVE our lives to God. This means surrendering everything: our will, our dreams, our desires, our relationships—everything to God.

I remember doing this at a very, very early age. I really hadn't committed horrible sins. But in my heart I felt guilty for the things I had done: the lies, disrespect to my mom, and bad attitudes in my heart. I knew I was displeasing God. I also knew, because I had been told almost from birth, that I needed to give my heart to God in order to receive forgiveness. I still remember sitting on my bed and thinking, "Here goes!" I remember praying something like this, "Dear Jesus, I know I have done things that are wrong. Please forgive me. Enter my heart. Forgive my sins. I want to give my life to you."

After praying this prayer I kept my eyes shut for a minute longer until I was ready. Then I opened them. I looked around my room and wondered what had changed. I sat there waiting for lighting to strike or thunder to sound. I just knew something weird was going to happen. But the room was quiet. Nothing was out of order. I assumed that I had done something wrong in the process, so I prayed again, "Lord Jesus. PLEEESE enter my heart. I want you to forgive me of my sins. In Jesus' name."

I looked up again. Still nothing. I was afraid I had "done it wrong." I had seen people in church cry and shake when they gave their hearts to Christ. But I didn't feel anything.

The truth is that on that ordinary day in Oxen Hill, MD, something huge happened. The Bible teaches us that the moment a person asks God to enter his or her life, the Holy Spirit of God begins to dwell within his or her spirit. The Bible says that He takes up residence. He is "sealed" inside of us. He NEVER will leave. This is what the Bible calls being "born again." Once a person is born, he or she never can be unborn. Over time Satan may lie to us and tell us that we've done something to remove the Holy Spirit from our lives, but this is a lie from hell. ONCE BORN, ALWAYS BORN.

The Bible says that when we accept Jesus into our lives, we become heirs with Him to eternal life.

What is the Holy Spirit doing in our lives? How does He dwell within our hearts? Why is this significant? The answer is deep but simple. He is there to teach us how to develop a relationship with God. John 17:3 says, "And this is eternal life, that they may know You, the only true God, and Jesus Christ whom You have sent."

Going back to the birth analogy, everyone has a different birthing story. Some of us were easy to deliver; we basically just crawled out of the womb on our own volition. Some of us struggled almost to the point of death. My daughter, Anna Katherine, fell somewhere in the middle of these two extremes. But at the end of the day the birth is just the beginning. The real relationship develops over time.

In the spiritual world this holds true. God delivered us to have an eternal relationship with Him. However, we only can fully enjoy this relationship by knowing God in a more and more intimate way. This is done through the work of the Holy Spirit. He is our teacher, our counselor, and sometimes our rebuker.

"But how, how, how? How does it all work? How can I hear the voice of God? How can I hear the voice of the Holy Spirit? Heck, I didn't even hear him when He entered into my life?" Seeking God can be a very frustrating experience. I remember having felt it in my own life. However, one of the greatest legacies my parents have left me is that they taught me how to hear the quiet voice of the Almighty God—how to hear the voice of the Holy Spirit who resides within my soul. The ability to hear God is not a skill; it is not a gift. It is a discipline.

Romans 12:1-2 says, "I beseech you therefore, brethren, by the mercies of God, that you present your bodies a living sacrifice, holy, acceptable to God, which is your reasonable service. And do not be conformed to this world, but be transformed by the renewing of your mind, that you may prove what is that good and acceptable and perfect will of God."

That last phrase of verse two reminds us what the Bible has taught us from the very beginning: God has a will, a plan, a laid-out path, for every one of us. AND, His will is good, acceptable, and perfect. God knows what He is doing in my life. He's got it all figured out for me. This is true, no matter how screwed up I think I have become. However, this verse also tells us how we can discover His will: "do not be conformed to this world, but be transformed BY THE RENEWING OF YOUR MIND."

RENEWING OF YOUR MIND. What does this mean? It means discipline. Avoid being carried away by the whims of television—the persuading influences of pop culture. Constantly renew your mind. But how does one do this?

"For the word of God is living and powerful, and sharper than any two-edged sword, piercing even to the division of soul and spirit, and of joints and marrow, and is a discerner of the thoughts and intents of the heart" (Heb. 4:12).

It boils down to the Bible—the Word of God. The secret to living intimately with Christ depends in a big way on our desire to pursue intimacy with Him through His Word. The Bible teaches repeatedly that God speaks through His Word. He teaches through His Word. He Guides through His Word. That's not to say that He cannot speak through other people, circumstances, and even dreams. From time to time He does just that, but the normal way that He desires to build intimacy with us is through His Word.

Many of us groan to hear such a disappointing answer: The Bible—that's so mundane. Over time, especially those who have been reared "Christian" have gotten used to seeing a dusty Bible on its top shelf or in a pew at a house of worship. We know it is God's Word, but it just seems, to be quite honest, so boring, confusing, and totally out of touch with anything going on in the world in which we live. Could it possibly even be out of date?

NO, NO, NO, NO! The Word of God is "living, and powerful." When God wants to paint for us a picture of the Bible, He uses the image of a sword. Not just any sword but a two-edged sword. This means it cuts both ways. At the time of the New Testament, this was one of the fiercest instruments of warfare. But how?

The image of a sword was not the image I conjured up when I first looked at my "NIV Children's Edition" Bible. It had colorful pictures between very difficult and sometimes difficult-to-understand stories. I still was in primary school when my father very lovingly taught me how to wield my weapon. He sat at our kitchen table and opened the Bible. He had lovingly inscribed it. He opened it, looked in my eyes, and told me if I would learn to hear from God, I always could succeed in life no matter what circumstances I faced. He taught me to listen to the voice of the Holy Spirit as He speaks through the sacred and inspired words of the Bible. This does not involve metaphysical gifts or religious training. To hear the voice of God requires time—time to be still and listen. It requires a person to pick up his or her Bible and be alone. It requires true meditation.

The key to hearing the voice of God is pausing from a hectic schedule to meditate on His Word. If we stop to listen, God will speak.

What happens is as follows:

Find a place in which you can be alone for at least 15 minutes. Sit down with your Bible and block out the world. Focus your mental energy on God, the Person, and on His Word—not on your problems and desires.

Jesus teaches us that when we want to approach the mighty throne of God, we fittingly and properly do so in a spirit of praise. Praise is a misused word that many church people associate with music. It is not music. It means FOCUS—focusing your mind on God and telling him why you love Him. For example, "God, I praise you because you always are near. I can feel your presence. I praise you because of your love. I know you love me." Begin your time with God by taking your mind off of yourself and focusing totally on who God is. This is praise. This is soul-cleansing.

The Bible then teaches us that after our minds have been turned to God, we can approach Him with all of our problems. The Bible says to "be anxious for nothing, but in everything by PRAYER and supplication, with thanksgiving, let your requests be made known to God; and the peace of God, which surpasses all understanding, will guard your hearts and minds through Christ Jesus" (Phil. 4:6-7). Every day we must take everything that bothers us, hurts us, concerns us, and causes us stress and lay it on an altar before God, our Father. Tell him your problems, your fears, your concerns, your sins—put everything before Him. God wants to be put in a position to solve our problems. He wants us to give Him our anxieties and to trust Him with the answers. In this very verse He promises that if we will surrender our concerns, a peace will surround us and guard our hearts and minds. In our hearts He will give us the guidance we desperately desire.

Then, after our hearts have been drawn to God and we have unloaded all of our burdens for the day, we humbly can voice a special request to God. Say something such as this, "Lord, now please speak to my heart."

The Bible teaches that the Holy Spirit of God then will use the Words of God on the page to speak to specific concerns and relevant issues pertaining to our lives and circumstances at that particular time. He guides our thoughts and prepares our hearts to receive what the Holy Spirit is saying.

Then open the Bible and begin to read. Since I was a little girl, I have tried to read the Bible from cover to cover, over and over again. In the course of my life, I have read the entire Bible many times; however, I do not try to read it through in any specified length of time. When I meditate on the Word of God, I do not speed-read. I just read God's Word, reread the parts that are confusing, and think about the meaning of each particular word or phrase. I read systematically a specific book from beginning to end, not just randomly opening the Bible to draw conclusions out of thin air. The Holy Spirit will not magically write words onto the page of the Bible. But He does teach me to apply to my situation the specific message of God's Word. The Bible speaks of the Holy Spirit opening the eyes of our hearts and enlightening us so that we can understand the hope to which He has called us. He does this through His Word.

The Spirit of wisdom and revelation teaches us to make sense of ancient texts. This is the amazing part about the Bible; the actual words are the same, but sometimes the Holy Spirit applies them to a myriad of modern circumstances.

Here's a personal example to show you what I'm talking about. In Romans 12:1, it reads, "I beseech you therefore, brethren, by the mercies of God, that you present your bodies a living sacrifice, holy, acceptable to God, which is your reasonable service."

I recall reading that verse during my high-school days. As I read, I heard this voice in my head, "Christy, present your body a living sacrifice. It must be holy. I want you to pay attention to the clothes that you wear. You recently bought a bikini. It's not ugly, but I don't think it is holy. Your body must be a sacrifice. Take it back." I remember this clearly because in this particular instance, I fussed and fumed. I didn't take it back. I kept it. In fact, not only did I keep it, I hid it in my suitcase for college. However, the Holy Spirit lives in my heart and wouldn't drop the issue. I couldn't quit thinking about that verse and ultimately wore the bikini only a few times. What a waste of money! I should have just taken it back.

This is how God works through His Word. The verse itself says nothing about bikinis. But the Holy Spirit dwells in my spirit. He applies the sacred words of Scripture to me in a way that is real, relevant, and easy to understand. Sometimes, like a two-edged sword, it penetrates to the inner parts of our hearts. Every time I wore that stupid bikini, I kept hearing His Words over and over again!

Quite possibly no other person reading Romans 12:1 ever will think about bikinis. I possibly won't either. It is the dynamic of a living and active relationship. The Holy Spirit knows where we are. He knows our hearts completely. He knows our secret struggles. He is the one person in the world who is free to talk to us about anything. This is His desire. This is intimacy.

Pray to God about the things in His Word that He has revealed to you. In this case, I don't remember exactly, but my prayer went something like this, "Lord, I don't want to take it back. It's just like Cristiana's. It's cute. Returning things in Brazil is complicated. I want to keep it. It's not fair." It may have been an immature conversation, but it was real to me. It was relevant. It was a daughter talking to her Father.

The amazing thing about our relationship with the Lord is that even if we fuss and fume, He responds in our hearts. Of course, I don't remember the exact words that I prayed to God that day, but I specifically remember the gist of His answer, "Christy, it's not about Cristiana. It's about you. Just trust me. Obey." I still remember this lesson.

Over the course of my life I have had thousands of dialogues with God the Father. Although saying this sounds surreal, we talk on a daily basis. Some of these conversations, such as the one about the bikini, have been goofy or mundane. Others, such as the dialogue I had with God after my mom died, were extremely meaningful. Although I am married and I love my husband and I have parents, brothers, and two beautiful daughters that I adore, the single most-important relationship in my life is not with any one of them. The single most-important, influential, and passionate relationship I have is with God, the Father.

I have learned that God, Our Father, is concerned with every detail of my life. The Bible says He's the Father of wisdom and wants to give it to us. He is the only person in the universe that actually knows the future. He always gives correct guidance; He wants to do just that. The problem is that most of us believe the most dangerous and seemingly innocuous lie to emerge from the pits of hell. We hear it in our heads and believe, "I can't hear God's voice." "I can't understand the Bible." "I don't have time to meditate." "I'm not the super-spiritual type." And so we live our lives in needless darkness. We make faulty decisions when we have a Counselor sealed inside our hearts.

Every day, we could, if we wanted to, hear the voice of the Almighty God, masterful Designer of the universe, speak to us and personally guide and direct every step of our lives. His desire as a loving Father is to help us avoid pitfalls, make good decisions, and show us what is in our hearts. He wants us to see others for what they really are and reveal to us whom we really can trust. He wants to lead us to the future and the hope He planned for us before we were born. But, like an ever-antsy toddler, we often struggle to sit still long enough to hear His voice.

This is the way life is meant to be lived—intimately with the Father. But intimacy requires effort. It requires time. We have to decide, *Do I want to be intimate with God in the way He wants to be intimate with me? Do I want to stop my life and listen to what He has to say? Do I want to know Him, His thoughts, His ways? Do I want to see the world as He does? Do I really want to be near to Him, since doing so will affect everything?*

John 17:3 says that we were given eternal life to KNOW HIM. We have been given the opportunity to have a unique and special relationship with God. We actually were created for this, but this, too, is a choice. If we dare to pursue intimacy with God, all other relationships will flow from this one, single, most-important relationship. He wisely will guide the course of our lives and bring us joy and meaning. He will lead us into the "good, acceptable and perfect will of God."

Value 3

Defining the Art of Self-Discipline

The story goes that my Great-Great-Great-Great-Grandfather Butler served as a butler at the Queen's court in England. His children immigrated to America and somehow landed in the Louisiana Delta. His grandson, my great-great-grandfather, was a private in the Confederate army during the Civil War. He left behind a son, Rupert Butler. Rupert became Dr. Rupert Butler, a distinguished country doctor who, in his horse-drawn buggy, made house calls all over north Louisiana. His daughter, Marjorie, was to become my beloved Grandmother Akins.

My mother's family, the Deakinses, are from the hills of the Smoky Mountains in a small community called Gray. In Gray, genealogy is best traced in old church cemeteries, where grandparents still take their grandchildren to visit the family plots, as they carefully place flowers and recall stories of lost loved ones. In Gray, family is precious and remembered, even if rarely famous.

Nothing is blue about my bloodline, no matter how it is traced. However, I could not be more proud of my heritage. God has blessed my family. Both sides of my family tree are comprised of God-fearing men and women for at least four generations, if not more. My family has a long history of people with deep moral character and conviction. They have been citizens of integrity. I am proud of the legacies I carry of family members from both ends of the South and the unique characteristics I have acquired from both. I'm proud of all these traits except, well, for one.

Once while visiting in Gray, I overheard a conversation among some distant relatives. Laughing among themselves they said, "You can always tell a Deakins when you see one. A Deakins always has bright blue eyes. A Deakins always has those high cheekbones." I have thought about that a lot. I would like to add a third defining characteristic of most Deakinses: a Deakins always will be the shortest person in the room.

My mother was born Sherry Jeanine Deakins, the oldest of three daughters born to J.E. and Louise Deakins. (J.E. literally is his name and not simply his initials. He jokes that since he was the ninth child, my great-grandmother exhausted her list of names!) All of their daughters and granddaughters are lovely. All of us for at least three generations have piercing blue eyes, distinctive cheek-bones, and beautiful smiles. And, what is most remarkable, in three generations, is that the tallest one of us is 5-foot-2.

I inherited many Deakins traits for which I am proud, but being 5-feet-and-one-half-inch tall (I always emphasize the one-half inch) has been the one I have enjoyed the least. In fact for years I wres-tled with God over this very issue. I thoroughly exhausted myself and never gained a millimeter for my efforts. Once, I actually went to a quack doctor who tried to stretch my bones.

I have not liked looking up to people. Until recently I have not liked appearing younger. I have not liked being unable to reach the top shelf of the kitchen cabinet without having to climb on top of the counter. However, these issues have paled in comparison to the most nagging and irritating aspect of being short: the constant battle of the bulge.

A short person has no room for eating binges of any kind. Every calorie shows up somewhere obvious. The body simply is too small to hide the fat. I discovered this when I hit puberty and my body filled out. I immediately began to notice that I would have to work to keep my weight down. My waist was not narrowing naturally like most of my scrawny, little Brazilian girlfriends. I couldn't just keep eating ice-cream and junk food like they did. The ugly truth was exposed. I was going to be a part of that large majority who struggles with weight throughout life.

My mother had fought her own weight battle since she was a little girl. As a result she had become somewhat "organic" before doing so was hip. She never nagged us to eat better or talked to us about weight issues. She discreetly reared us on carefully balanced menus and encouraged us to be active. Since we were young children, she gave us skim milk for breakfast, cooked wheat bread almost daily from scratch, hunted down carob-covered raisins for desert, and boiled vegetables instead of frying them (which is not natural for a country girl to do). She never once suggested anyone go on a diet. In fact dieting wasn't an issue, because none of us really ever needed one. She did not try to control my eating, nor did she force me to exercise. She just prepared healthy meals, went jogging herself every morning, and let me duke it out with my body, while she set a positive example.

Over the course of my adolescence, my weight went back and forth as I figured out how to balance my eating and exercise habits with my emotional state of mind. I never really was heavy, but I also never really was really skinny. Somehow in my distorted psyche, this bothered me. I tried fad diets, diet pills, and calorie counting on tiny kitchen scales. Although I thankfully never fell prey to any definable eating disorder, my eating was discernably off-balance. For most of my teen-age and college years, eating was an increasingly consuming obsession. It was a challenge—one in which everyone could see whether I was winning or losing.

The worse weight defeat I ever suffered was the summer before I went to college. For me the transition was titanic. In June I graduated from my miniscule international school in urban Brazil. By August I was expected to be nicely established in rural Arkansas, a state I never had visited and often confused with Alabama. I had a lot to learn. Even my fashion sense was all wrong.

As a way of transitioning me to life in America, my parents decided to take our family to live with my Mamaw and Papaw Deakins in Gray for four weeks before school started in the fall. As little kids my brothers and I had spent lots of time there and loved their farm. Besides adjusting to American life in general, the specific goal for this trip was to teach me how to drive the 1987 red Nissan Sentra my parents had bought me for school. I was 17 years old and didn't have a learner's permit.

I pretended that all was well, but in fact I was struggling to keep it together. All summer I mulled over my loss and my new life. In fact the horrible jerks and twists I created as I tried to cope with the Sentra's stick shift turned out to be very symbolic of the mess I was feeling on the inside. I never had the nerve to admit anything to my parents, but I was grieving. I wasn't as tough as I was pretending to be. I was depressed and angry at God for making me have to make this break from my life as a missionary kid in Brazil. Brazil was the world I knew; now I was leaving it.

In the end I did spend a lot of time practicing my driving that summer. I drove up and down Papaw's driveway and released the clutch over and over again until I could do it without killing the car. I drove over the hills in my Uncle David's cow pasture so I could get comfortable with the gas pedal. Sometimes my parents even let me on the road. But unfortunately for me, the rest of my time was spent in Mamaw's kitchen. There I self-indulged in the myriad of country delicacies that constantly emerged from her veteran oven. During those four weeks I put on 20 pounds as I ate homemade ice cream, oatmeal cookies, banana pudding, and yeast rolls. I graduated from high school weighing 110 pounds. I showed up at the college freshman retreat topping a whopping 130. I had unbelievably succeeded in consuming three-quarters of a pound in excess of what I was burning EVERY SINGLE DAY! I felt like a wrecked car. I spent the next two years wearing Umbros with elastic waistbands and sweat pants trying to camouflage all those ridiculous pounds. I had self-indulged horribly and paid a high price for it. While most of my friends were being asked out on blind dates, I was power-walking in the dark around and around the campus. I was counting mileage and, ounce by ounce, slowly dropping the excess weight.

The lesson of self-discipline was an extremely difficult lesson. In retrospect the Lord clearly used my struggle with weight to teach me the valuable lesson on how to discipline myself. This carried over into other more critical areas of life. However, oh how, I wish I had learned it an easier and less humiliating way!

I wish I had paid more attention to one of the most important legacies my mother ever left me. I remember her talking to me about it in the car one day as we drove from Little Rock to Arkadelphia where I attended college. The words she spoke to me that day were not necessarily enlightening. What mattered was the fact that she was verbalizing something I had seen her practice since my earliest memories. "Christy," she said, "when God created us, he created us with a body, a spirit, and a soul. Our soul is made up of our mind, our emotions, and our will. We must allow the Holy Spirit to penetrate our soul and control our will. If we do not, our flesh will take control of our body, our emotions, and our minds." My mother was one of the most Spirit-controlled women I have ever known. Some people call this godliness, but it was her discipline. She allowed God to control her mind, body, and spirit. I had seen this for years. Although she probably did so imperfectly at times, I knew she was living the life God had designed for her to live. As I listened to her talk, I clearly could see the stark contrast of her disciplined direction with the chaotic mess I had created that summer after high school.

Each part of our being must be disciplined by God Himself, or our lives will spin out of control as my weight did in those short weeks before college. Our bodies must be disciplined, our minds must be disciplined, and our emotions must be disciplined. This is a lesson that can take a lifetime to master, but it is important. It is a skill that cannot really be taught in a classroom or in a church building but one that God intends to burn within each of us through the bumps in life as He painstakingly teaches us how to surrender our lives to Him. It determines personal success that will last through this age and into the next age more than will talent, privilege of birth, or wealth. This is the lesson of self-discipline.

SELF-DISCIPLINE. It is the discipline of our very essence. When I think of discipline, I always think about the lumps and bumps that surround my gut. But that is because that was one of the means God is using to discipline me. The truth is that we are not primarily flesh. First and foremost we are spiritual entities. More to being human exists than flesh, blood, and hormones. In Genesis 2 the Bible teaches us that He created man out of the dust of the earth and that He created woman from man. In this way we are organic. However, being organic is not being alive. We can embalm our bodies to keep them around for quite a while, but this does not keep anyone alive. For a person to live, God breathed into that individual the breath of life—the "divine spark." God gave us a spirit. He made us not only alive but altogether unique, unlike anything else that He has created, at least on earth. He created us with a soul, or "psyche" as the Greeks called it. Our "psyche" is that part of us that cannot be seen: our software. For example when a brain surgeon cuts open someone's head, he cannot see the person's thoughts, feelings, or choices. This stuff composes our "psyche." Some have said that our "psyche" has three parts: our mind, our heart, and our will. But our psyche alone does not make us human. Once our daughters had a poodle named Sandy. Sandy had a mind, a heart and, being female, DEFINITELY a will all her own. Still she was in no way human. What makes us human is not our "psyche" but our spirit.

Our spirit is the part of us that God originally gave us. It represents the innerworking of our being that knows that God exists and that life is bigger than are the actions of people. It is the part of us that can make moral judgments and conscious decisions. It is the part of us that has the ability to communicate with God. It is the part that makes us eternal beings and gives us an inner awareness of our own immortality.

The Bible teaches us that originally humanity did not know evil. At least on earth, evil did not exist except as an untested possibility. The human spirit was flawless and made in the image of the Spirit of God. Because the human spirit was good, so were the mind, will, and heart. Even the human body was perfect. Death did not exist. Humanity did not know corruption.

However, the Bible quickly injects that the Garden of Eden was temporary. No one really knows how long it did last, but eventually the people that existed corrupted themselves and the world around them. They surrendered to the temptation to allow a wrongful ambition into their hearts. Just as Anakin Skywalker wanted to be more than just a servant to the Republic, the first people wanted not to be created in the image of God. They wanted to BE God. Adam and Eve chose to challenge God. They tested the theory of evil.

When this happened, the nature of being human changed. The spirit of humanity eternally was corrupted. Death penetrated the spirit of humanity. The Bible says that we became "slaves to sin." It is a confusing assertion, but in my mind, I can picture it best with the admittedly imperfect analogy of a car. My body is my car. We can fix it up, soup it up, or let it go to pot, but it cannot do anything on its own. It is just an outside shell. When God originally created this "car", He gave it a driver—our Spirit—and three passengers. One passenger is our mind; another, our heart; and, of course, our wills are the navigators.

With the fall of Adam, a big, creepy, ugly thug jumped in the back seat to become the fourth passenger and to forever influence the rest of the car. The Bible calls it our "flesh." As sons and daughters of Adam, we are born slaves to the guy in the backseat. He is the ultimate liar and nagger. After a while we cannot help but obey what he tells us to do. He tricks, bullies, and eventually dominates our minds, our emotions, and our will.

Even the most self-controlled of all people cannot resist the influence and pressure of the Flesh. George Lucas personifies the transition better than anyone when he portrays this transformation through the character of Anakin Skywalker. When evil entered his spirit, it became his master; even the most talented and promising Jedi could not resist. Anakin became Darth Vader. The only difference between Anakin and the rest of us is that with most of us, the transition is slower and more well-disguised.

One evening, when my daughters still were in preschool, we lay in bed at bedtime. I was reading a Bible story. The story happened to be about Adam and Eve in the garden of Eden. Trying to make the story as interesting as possible, I began to imitate the characters in the familiar story.

"Adam and Eve, you cannot eat the fruit of the tree of the knowledge of good and evil," I said in the deepest and mightiest voice I could muster. "So, as time went by, a serpent came slithering through the garden up to Eve."

I suddenly changed my voice into a highly seductive Angelina Jolie-type voice and said, "Should you really not eat that fruit? It is so, so, SO delicious. It will make you so smart. Why don't you eat just a little piece?" I turned and gave my girls a sweet, coquettish smile.

At this point in the story I stopped telling the story and asked my daughters the following question: "Girls, what do you think Eve should do?"

Elizabeth, the younger of the two, screamed out as loud as she could, "EAT IT!"

To her it seemed natural. To our natural person, the flesh is by far and away the strongest influence in our inner being. It eventually will cause us to experience the world as it determines for us to experience it. We will feel the emotions that it wants us to feel; it will allow us to intellectually interpret things the way it wants us to interpret them. Ultimately it will make the choices that determine who we are.

In Romans 6-8 the apostle Paul explains this. The flesh is the very reason giving our lives to Christ as early as possible is important. When Christ died on the cross, He died to get rid of the influence of our flesh. He died so we could choose to be free from this: "knowing this, that our old man was crucified with Him, that the body of sin might be done away with, that we should no longer be slaves of sin" (Rom. 6:6). Going back to the Anakin Skywalker analogy, Christ died, so we can take off our Vader mask and see the world and our life for what it really is: without the distorted interpretation of our flesh. Except in the real world, taking off the mask is how we LIVE.

However, just accepting Christ into one's heart is not a magic potion that cures all issues involving the soul, but it is the all-important first step. Without this first step, Christ can't help us do anything. Referring back to the car analogy, when we ask Christ to enter our lives and the Holy Spirit begins to live within us, we, in effect, turn on the global positioning system or the cell phone. We can see where we're supposed to be going. We have the means to direct us and make the right choices at each and every turn.

The art of self-discipline begins at this point. Once we allow Christ inside the car, He begins the lifelong process of teaching us the art of staying in control of the wheel of that car. It is the art of ignoring the annoying banter of our flesh that tells us to indulge, indulge, INDULGE in one short-sighted venture after another. It is the art of not allowing him to control our emotions and how we feel about the circumstances in life and the multitudes of people that enter it. It is the art of intellectually understanding the complexities of the world without falling prey to our arrogant attitudes of self-sufficiency and self-righteousness.

In Romans 6:12-13 the Apostle Paul describes it like this, "Therefore do not let sin reign in your mortal body, that you should obey it in its lusts. And do not present your members as instruments of unrighteousness to sin, but present yourselves to God as being alive from the dead, and your members as instruments of righteousness to God. For sin shall not have dominion over you, for you are not under law but under grace." These verses may seem too "devotional" to understand, but they issue a monumental challenge, "Live above the flesh." It is a burden that seems impossible, especially in a complex, modern world. But the verse ends with a timeless promise that can be applied to every aspect of our being: "Sin shall NOT have dominion over you, for you are not under law but under grace." We are free! We have been given free will. We are made in the image of God. Through His grace we are free to choose to begin to make the right choices. We can have victory in our lives. We can defeat gluttony, lust, depression, or fear. In Christ, we can have control over our minds, over our emotions, and over our bodies. We can live the life God meant for us to live since the beginning of time. But how?

Value 4

Defeating the Flesh

For the most part, as I grew up, I was a very obedient and conscientious daughter. My brothers were the ones that usually got the spankings. Not me! However, as I got older, I found myself always clashing with my mother over my curfew. She insisted that I be in the house by 9 on school nights and 11 on weekends. That schedule may not sound unreasonable, but I believed I had extenuating circumstances. After all, I was in Brazil. The legal driving age is 18. Because of this nobody in high school drives a car. When we wanted to go out (which was every single weekend), we had to rely on public transportation. On weekends the bus would run in our neighborhood only every 30 to 45 minutes. This meant that if I were to arrive home safely before my curfew, the latest I could stay anywhere was 10. This counted the time it took to walk to the bus stop and wait on the bus.

What further complicated the situation in my mind was that Brazilians are notoriously nocturnal. They don't get showered and out of the house before 9 p.m. I believed I always was missing the best parts of the parties. This bothered me to no end. I constantly begged my mother to extend my curfew. My mother, who had been reared to believe that "nothing good ever happens after 11", stood her ground. Attempting to protect my virtue, she refused to let me stay out late. We argued constantly over this issue, but in four years I never made any headway. So, in an attempt to treasure every possible millisecond before 11 p.m., I would make my best estimate of what time the bus to my neighborhood would pull to the stop. I then made a mad dash for it. Half the time I missed the 10:30 bus and chased it down in my four-inch heels. Some girls stagger home after curfew because they've had too much to drink. I staggered in because my heels were ruined from sprinting on cobblestone. Sadly enough, I was grounded for about 50 percent of my high school career. In fact, I defiantly blew my curfew my last night in Brazil and ironically was grounded when I got on the airplane to leave the country.

When I arrived in the U.S. and showed up at Ouachita Baptist University, the first thing that actually excited me was the news that this very year the college had been forced to revoke a 100-year-old curfew. This truly was a stroke of good fortune. When my parents dropped me off at school, for the first time in my life I had no one there to tell me when I had to go to my room and when I had to turn off the light. I had been freed. It felt intoxicating! My very first night on campus, I borrowed a car (Dad had mine until they returned to Brazil) at 11 o'clock and drove all over Arkadelphia, AR. Honestly, doing this wasn't very much fun, since Arkadelphia really never has anything to do after 11 p.m, but I still felt an air of exhilaration. My mother's oppression had ended!

I walked into my dorm that evening to discover that I was not the only one enjoying release from parental shackles of bondage. Not only were every light on and every door open, the pizza man stood in the lobby unloading a three-foot stack of pizza boxes onto the counter. We all were living high on fraternity mixers and campus welcome events! Not until mid-terms did most of us freshmen girls even realize we were at college to do anything but party.

Life was glorious as it settled into a somewhat ridiculous "routine." A few lucky girls would go out with the upperclassmen. But until late in the evening the bulk of us lurched around campus or at coffee shops looking for boys. Then we'd mosey home to our oversized T-shirts and facial mud to eat pizza, talk about boys, and scan textbooks for the subtitles of our long reading assignments. We consistently showed up late for class but never missed lunch at "Walt's" cafeteria. There we'd dine on our typical meal of "Captain Crunch" and TCBY frozen yogurt and scan for new material for our evening hallway "gossipfest." It was silly. It was fun. In some ways life began taking a surreal turn for the better.

However, after about a month of this reckless irresponsibility, I clearly saw I would not be able to survive four years of this kind of living. I had used up all my tardies for class. I already had missed my full quota of daily quizzes. My weight still was climbing. Besides that, ugly black lines were finding permanent residence under my eyes. I was sleeping less than three hours per night.

My lifestyle had spiraled into an undisciplined, out-of-control spin. I was sleeping at odd hours of the day. I ate irregularly and only food that had been manufactured thousands of miles away. My only consolation was to discover that I wasn't the only one in this situation. My newfound friends all were on the verge of collapse. We had celebrated freedom long enough. A few of the girls already were on academic probation. Something had to give.

Being "master of my domain" and in total control, I decided to become a "self-disciplined" person and make the necessary changes. Obviously the first step involved swallowing my pride and creating a personal curfew. I abandoned my 2 a.m. routine and began to slither back into my dorm sometime after the library closed at 10 p.m. I needed to study; I needed to sleep. But as I drifted back to the real world and looked into my full-length mirror, I realized I still had a major problem: 20 bulging pounds still stared back at me. In fact, in those first weeks of school, I had added an extra seven pounds. My figure was beginning to resemble an old-timey alarm clock instead of an hourglass. How was I ever going to get this under control? Leaving punctually from the library was not going to fix this. Having been through years of off-and-on dieting, I knew that this was a problem greater than myself. In high school I had enough trouble losing two or three pounds. How was I ever going to lose 27 pounds of lard if I had no kitchen scale, no diet pills, nor even a mother to drag me out of bed for early-morning jogs? I would have to lose weight by myself. I would have to do it on a diet of institutional food. I was going to have to exercise rigorously and alone. This realization was enough to break me. I felt despair. I knew the truth. I just didn't have enough discipline within myself to take me where I needed to go.

My self-sufficiency was depleted. Only then was I willing to look within myself—not to my arrogant inner-strength, but to the Holy Spirit of God Who quietly had been waiting to take the wheel of the car. He knew I was desperately trying to fit in and make friends. He knew I wanted more than anything to find a niche. He knew I wanted to go out on real dates. He knew I didn't want to be fat. He also knew that I, Christy Renee Akins, had no way to make that happen.

I remember one night very specifically, I was in a phone booth in the Flippin-Perrin girls' dormitory. I felt horrible—not just because of the weight. I was lonely, fat, and tired. The new and improved "self-disciplined Christy" only was slightly better than the previous version. I sat in the phone booth for a while and then dialed my parents' number. I wanted to quit. I wanted to go home. As I sat there, I silently heard in my spirit the quiet voice of God saying to me, "Don't quit. When am I going to take over again?" I felt His presence. The phone rang on the other end. My mother picked up. She said "hello"; I said nothing. I hung up the phone and went to my room. I wasn't being "superspiritual." At that time I wasn't even involved in church. But I consciously decided to let Him control me. I needed to get my heart, my body, and my will back in submission to the Lord. That day I learned that the heart of self-discipline was not my alarm clock or the bathroom scale. It wasn't even inner-strength and intense willpower. The secret to living a disciplined life is living a life that is submitted to God's control.

To speak frankly, self-discipline never is enough. No one can master one's flesh. Too many angles exist: weight, sex drive, intellect, emotions, and on the list goes. Everyone has an Achilles heel. Our inner being is too sophisticated to master it all. Submission is required. Through submission to the Lord our lives become disciplined. He is the one that does the disciplining. He's the only one who can deal with all the complexity of our souls. On that day sitting in the phone booth of the Flippin-Perrin dorm, I did not decide to buck up and try harder. I already had gone about as far as I could take myself. My "self-control" was doing nothing but making me a more dressed-up manatee instead of transforming me completely into a sleek and agile dolphin. The decision was to quit trying to be the boss and instead to submit completely to the direction and leadership of the Lord—listen, trust, obey, and go wherever that would take me.

I had to re-instigate my "quiet time." When I was a young girl, my parents had nurtured in me the habit of spending time daily with the Lord and meditating on His Holy Word. I can't realistically remember when I started reading my Bible before I went to bed, but somehow that summer before college, in my anger, that activity had stopped. After the aborted phone call home, I went to Wal-Mart and bought a spiral notebook in which I could write down spiritual truths and record specific prayer requests. At this point my spirit was not in submission to the Lord. But I knew that if I would sit still and listen to Him, He would guide my thoughts, my actions, my attitudes, my heart, and the thing that unfortunately concerned me the most: my body.

As my quiet time got off the ground, the Lord began helping me organize my time. He gave me ideas as to how to organize my schedule. Every day as I sat with my opened Bible and meditated on His Words, I received new strength and determination to make the right choices. Each day the world looked a little different to me than it had the day before.

I began to take off work around 4:30. If I brought my running clothes with me to the office, I could go running almost uninterrupted for the next hour. I could be back in the cafeteria by 5:45 p.m.—time enough to goof off for a couple of hours and catch some time with the cute freshmen boys before I had to buckle down, study, and head to my room for my quiet time. Sometimes I could find someone to run with me, but most of the time, I went by myself. This was going to be my basic routine for the next year and a half. I began to formulate a plan. I began to have hope instead of despair. The task was not going to be easy, but little by little, I felt His assurance that the weight was going to be removed.

My situation was not just a matter of exercise and routine. The physical was just the beginning. My spirit had to be harnessed. My anger had to be released. I submitted control of my life back to the Lord because I recognized I needed help getting my body back. However, the Lord had a higher purpose. He let my body spin out of my control so I would recognize what He already knew: I needed Him involved in every area of my life. I was about to make some of the most important decisions of my life: whom to love, where to live, what to become. I was not prepared. I needed my heavenly Father.

God desires that each of us realize that we must live our lives in submission to the Lord. The Spirit of God must totally control us. This never is easy. No one wants to give up control. We are all "control freaks"—born wanting to be in charge of our destinies and usually the destinies of those around us. We naturally are greedy for power.

We are tempted with the lie of Eve. In our heart our flesh seduces us as it whispers, "You CAN be like God." "You DESERVE to be in charge! You can have IT ALL!" We somehow believe that we'll be better off—happier and more successful—if we do things our way instead of God's way. In our human flesh, submitting to God is unnatural. Our flesh naturally is in rebellion against God.

The "I'm-smart-enough-to-be-happy" attitude, however, is a lie. As contradictory as things may seem, the truth is that our own happiness and our success ultimately will NOT depend on how gifted we are. It will not depend on how beautiful, thin, smart, rich, powerful, or talented we are. The concept seems almost boring, but our own long-term happiness actually will depend on how submitted we live to the Spirit of God.

Over and over again the Bible illustrates this. We see people who truly are successful. We see others who are miserable failures. We see men and women who seem to achieve life's pinnacle of success, only to fall prey to merciless depression and loss. We see others who are contradictorily happy in spite of their circumstances.

For me two biblical superheroes really illustrate what God can do through those who faithfully submit to Him. One is Joseph, the other is Moses—both princes of Egypt and servants of the living God. Both were highly successful. Both possess bizarre stories of success that only can be attributed to obeying God's plan for their lives.

Joseph was the twelfth son of Israel, a successful sheep farmer in the Middle East and heir of Abraham. The Bible does not describe Joseph as smarter, braver, or more successful than any of his brothers—only that he was his father's favorite. Israel taught his sons to honor the true God, but Joseph seems like a spoiled kid who doesn't know when to keep his mouth shut. He pushes his brothers' buttons and continually spouts off dreams to annoy his already resentful brothers. Eventually, his brothers plot to get rid of him and actually sell him to slavetraders headed for Egypt.

At this point Joseph must have felt as though his life was over. He had bigger problems than I did in being a chubby freshman. For him this had to be one of life's true low points. We only can imagine what went on in Joseph's head as, with chains around his neck and ankles, he marched down the dusty road under the merciless Sahara sun. Was it God's fault that this had happened to him? God certainly allowed him to go through this. God certainly could have stopped this at some point. Did God deserve to be the Lord of his life if that is what He was going to do with it?

Joseph made the remarkable and surprising decision to allow God to control his already-messed-up life. The Bible tells us that when he was sold as a slave, "The Lord was with him and that the Lord made all he did to prosper in his hand." Although no one possibly could enjoy slavery, under the circumstances, Joseph was doing OK. Apparently he felt God's presence and during his slavery lived for the Lord.

However, the story unbelievably takes a turn for the worse. Potiphar, the guy that bought Joseph, has a desperate housewife who wants to sleep with Joseph. Joseph is a young, single male who easily could have justified this one little indiscretion. In fact this woman is in a position to boost his personal position. But he chooses to allow God's Spirit to guide him. He actually runs away from a beautiful and powerful and potentially naked woman. In what shortsightedly could have felt like divine betrayal, God's intention is not to spare Him the consequences of turning down this woman's advances. She has him thrown into prison for trumped-up, attempted rape charges. Joseph would stay in prison for years.

Of course, I don't know this, but at this point in his life, being a human, perhaps he once again faced the eternal questions of life: *WHAT AM I DOING SERVING A GOD THAT ALLOWS THIS TO HAPPEN TO ME? If He's truly the God of the universe, why am I being made to go through this? All the evil people are winning at life. Wouldn't I be better off if I just did my own thing? At least I wouldn't be in prison. I could be in Potiphar's bed right now. Surely I could do better than this for my life!*

We have no way of knowing what goes through Joseph's head at this time, but we do know this: he doesn't rebel against the Lord. He continues to live in submission to God. The Bible says that "the LORD was with him, and whatever he did, the LORD made it prosper." After years of living in the underworld, Joseph experiences God's miraculous reversal of fortunes in his life. He becomes one of the principal players at a critical moment in Egyptian history. Joseph has an encounter with Pharaoh and helps him survive a devastating famine. Through this relationship Joseph becomes the second most-powerful man in all of Egypt, the superpower of the ancient world. He fathers not one but two of the 12 tribes of Israel. Some even believe he is a type of Christ figure. The end of the story is as glorious as the beginning is ghastly. But God's plan never was even explained to Joseph. It was completely concealed in the midst of the mess.

God does not promise to ensure a powerful political career to everyone who obeys Him. That is not the lesson of Joseph. But one can fairly say this: Joseph had no way of knowing what God was doing or wanted to do with his life. At some point in his early years, he committed to serve the Lord no matter what the consequences. This decision to submit to the Lord's will would prove to be the deciding factor throughout his life. God spent years discipling Joseph in preparation for greatness. God could trust Joseph to be true. Because of this faithful submission Joseph was privileged to affect all of human history. He was one of the founding fathers of the nation of Israel.

The story of Moses is just as amazing. He springs from nowhere. His mother is nothing more than a slave who wrecklessly puts her baby in the Nile as she attempts to save his life. He miraculously is discovered by Pharoah's daughter and is adopted to be her son despite the prejudice against his race. For 40 years Moses is reared with a silver spoon in his mouth. He is royalty. He is a prince. We could speculate that his birth mother, who is hired as his nurse, teaches him about God. However, we have no indication that Moses is a spiritual giant. He appears to be an angry and undisciplined man who kills an Egyptian guard on an impulse. Because of the murder charges, Moses flees the greatest country in the world to get lost in the wilderness. He marries the daughter of an insignificant sheepherder and proceeds to spend the next 40 years in the mountains as he works for his father-in-law. Some would say that, in itself, is a fate worse than death!

But then something happens. He meets God, or rather, God meets Him. God tells him that He has a special plan for his life. God tells him that He can use him. Moses feels like a total loser and tells this to God. He says, "I'm not your man. I'm a screwball. I'm not even an average speaker. I'm not good enough to do anything for God."

God answers him in a way that Scripture records to speak to us all. God said to Moses, "I will certainly be with you."

At this point, Moses has to decide if he will go out on that most extended and uncertain of all limbs. Is he going to trust God? He can go back to his wife and his herd and live out the rest of his days with the sheep, or He can live the life God is calling him to live and return to Egypt to face his former family—only this time, to challenge them. He can submit to God's will, or he can rebel and do his own thing. Fortunately for all humanity, Moses made the right choice.

All of us, no matter who we are, sooner or later will face this question. *Who will be the boss? Who will determine what happens in my life?*

Godly self-discipline is nothing less than submitting daily to God's plan for our lives. But submitting to God's plan ultimately will determine more than exercise. When we choose to seek Him and obey, he disciplines our minds to be capable of understanding

54

things the way He sees them. This affects our careers, our goals, our dreams. He disciplines our hearts so that we love the things that He loves and despise the things that he despises. This determines our love lives, social choices, financial decisions, and circles of friends. He disciplines our wills, so that we can make the difficult and maybe even painful choices that He wants us to make through the leading of His Spirit—God's Holy Spirit. Submission plays itself out daily in the small things, but in God's hands nothing is small. Everything is defining. He disciplines us like a coach does an athlete harping at the details and preparing the champion. Although the process goes on until we reach eternity, our lives in God's hands always will be victorious.

At the end of my four years of college I graduated *magna cum laude* and was married seven days later. I weighed 105 pounds.

Value 5

Running from Rebellion

Rebellion is defined as "resistance to or defiance of any authority or control."

The opposite of submission is rebellion. This word has, at least in my mind, romanticized itself into being synonymous with freedom. After all, who doesn't love James Dean, Marlon Brando, or Bart Simpson? However, if we are talking about our relationship with God, rebellion is an insidious venom. Rebelling against God never ever results in anything except pain.

I know two young men. They were born in the same year and were from the same town. They grew up in very normal, active lifestyles. Both were born into good, middle-class families. Both were reared by two parents at home who loved them. They both were model children who faithfully attended church, demonstrated leadership, and were the apples of their parents' eyes. They also both loved soccer.

However, as they metamorphosed into young adults, their paths began to diverge. The first young man was the Brad Pitt of his generation. He was charming, intelligent, and an extremely good-looking student who also turned out to be a gifted athlete. He made his school's varsity squad and was chosen to be on select teams. He always had a beautiful girl on his arm. He spent his formative years traveling around his native country winning soccer championships and charming women. In fact he won for himself a four-year scholarship to a reputable university.

The other young man's growing-up years were a lot more challenging. He, too, was a very good-looking, intelligent young man with a penchant for sports. However, when he was a young child, his mother began to notice that he continued to demonstrate difficulty in school, even though she knew her son was smart. After years of frustrating tests, a diagnosis finally was made. This young man had a disability. Learning in school was especially a challenge. In fact, some people suggested he wouldn't even finish high school. This young man, although a good athlete, did not have time to try out for selective teams. He didn't travel around the country. Instead he spent his high-school years working, coaching children for church and community teams, and staying up late at night studying for high-school exams. He was a diligent worker and enjoyed life, but he learned early-on to never take anything for granted. He developed an indomitable spirit of determination.

As the two young men continued to grow up, one of them made a decision to submit to the Lord. One of them gave His life to the Lord's control and became an instrument of righteousness. The other one made the ever-popular decision that he would be better off on his own. Surprisingly the one that had received the most "blessings" from God was not the one that chose to submit to God. It was the other who understood his need for a Lord. It was the one who understood that He needed God's Spirit to guide him.

The first young man went to college on the sports scholarship. He dropped out after one year and transferred to a second school. At this school he partied and started to make failing grades. He hung in long enough to finish a successful sports season. Academics didn't seem important anyway in view of the celebrity promise of a sports career. He was on top of the world until one day he was arrested on drug charges. Things went from bad to worse when his drug problem eventually led to his dismissal from school. The young man packed his bags for home, in disgrace, with no degree and carrying the news that he was going to be the father of a baby conceived in his careless lifestyle. Before long this young man, in utter despair, attempted to commit suicide. How did things turn so fast? Recovery would take years

The second young man did not go off to elite schools. Instead he stayed at home and attended a local community college. He continued to help his dad on the farm and increased his volunteer involvement in his local church and community for social outlets. Throughout high school, this young man developed an interest in choir and had begun to train his voice. He turned out to be one of those unusual people God blessed with perfect pitch. He became a favorite at his church. Other churches in the area began to invite him to sing. He recorded a CD and soon became the church choir director. Defiantly beating all odds, he graduated from college and is pursuing a successful career.

What was the difference between these two very similar men? In a word: rebellion.

The flesh in all of us is born to rebel against our Maker. Our sin nature inside tells us to abandon God's rule of our lives and live life as we see fit. Usually sometime between the ages of 13 and 25, we all are tempted to do just that. Each of us consciously or subconsciously evaluates his or her life and makes a decision as to who will run it: God or self. Although those of us with greater challenges would seem to be more likely to rebel against a God who let these things happen to us; the opposite is true. Those who have more natural talent, more money, more beauty, more intelligence, or more opportunity somehow think that these things will take us further than will the God who gave us these blessings. We think that if we obey God, He will make us be poor. He will make us unsuccessful professionally. He won't let us have any fun. He'll probably never allow us to enjoy a meaningful romance. Our lives will somehow consist of a boring series of monotone church services that will lead us toward a life in a monastery, where we will spend the rest of our days wearing ugly brown robes, fasting, praying, and eventually dying virginal.

No better illustration of this exists than in the biblical pages of the book of Judges. If a guy ever existed that could be called a "man's man", it was Samson. When God created Samson, he created the biblical version of Bob Incredible. The guy was amazing. With his bare hands he could kill a lion. He could singlehandedly kill 1,000 seasoned warriors with a donkey jawbone. He was smart. For 20 years he judged the people of Israel. But Samson was an arrogant rebel. He mistakenly thought that God needed him more than he needed God. He chased foreign women who served other gods. This was something God specifically had instructed His people never to do. He shacked up with Delilah, a playgirl from the tribe of his worst enemy. Then in his arrogance, he told her the source of his strength. The question that I have asked myself since I, as a little girl, first heard this story, is, "Why did Samson tell Delilah his secret?" He obviously was a smart guy. He obviously didn't trust Delilah. Twice before she had betrayed him. Why would the leader of a country allow himself to be put into such a position? The answer, of course, is subjective. No one really knows for sure what he was thinking. Maybe it was just pillowtalk. But, I do have an opinion: rebellion. Samson really didn't think his strength emanated from his hair. After all those years of being "The Man", could he possibly no longer believe that his strength was in God's hands? Did he think that HE was the tough guy? In my opinion he thought he was enough.

The day Delilah gave him up, the Philistines poked out Samson's eyes and sent him to prison, where he spent possibly up to a few years shackled in bronze fetters and working as a grinder. In the blindness of prison Samson finally conceded to God's right to rule his life. In prison he fell, not into rebellion as he had lived his free days, but into submission to the Lord. At some point the Philistines decided to have a massive party in honor of Dagon, their god. As part of the celebration, perhaps to mock the Hebrews, they called up Samson, the longtime symbol of Hebrew strength. He was to perform for the amusement of the worshipers of Dagon. We don't know what kind of performance Samson was called on to do, but we do know that at some point during his act, he called on the Lord. He asked God to grant him the mercy to finish the job that God had called him to do when Samson was a child. That task was to free the Israelites from the rule of the Philistines. In one stroke of vengeance Samson—in superhero form—pushed the supporting pillars of the temple and killed more people that one day than he did in his entire career as a warrior. He paid a high price for his rebellion. His life did not turn out the way God would have chosen.

But Samson is not alone in the list of persons God blessed but who rebelled against Him. In fact, if, in all of history, one person who really blew it ever existed, this would not be Samson. If I were to make a list of the biggest disappointments in the Bible, Solomon would be up at the top. He was the ultimate "brat packer" or "milk-and-cookies" boy. His mother was Bathsheba, a woman so beautiful that David murdered a decorated soldier to have her. His father was King David, the man God chose to be eternally associated with the human blood line of Jesus. Then God chose Solomon himself among a multitude of siblings to be His choice as the future king of Israel. Humanly speaking, you couldn't think one could get luckier than this. But Solomon did. Not long after he began to reign as king over all of Israel, God Himself appeared to him and offered him anything in the world that he wanted. I can't possibly conceive of such an experience, but Solomon met God and spoke with Him in a way that pleased God. He asked God for wisdom—to rule His country with God's vantage point. God granted him his request; Solomon became the wisest man that has ever walked the face of the earth. But, God did more than that. He blessed Solomon financially and politically. He became famous. He became the richest man in the world. The Bible says, "King Solomon surpassed all the kings of the earth in riches and wisdom" (1 Kings 10:23). But as his kingdom expanded, his heart departed from the Lord.

For even though Solomon had wisdom straight from the throne of heaven, His heart and body regressed deeper and deeper into rebellion. Over time he began to indulge in sexual promiscuity. His spirit was not submitted to the Lord. He became controlled by his flesh. Solomon had 700 wives—princesses from all over the world. He had 300 concubines. He loved them; they turned his heart from the Lord. Somehow, he rebelled against the God who had appeared to him and who offered him the world. He rejected the One who had given him everything. Instead he had altars to false idols and high places to which his own children were taken to be sacrificed to evil idols. The Bible says, "Solomon did evil in the sight of the Lord" (1 King 11:6).

At the end of his life, we find that Solomon has become a miserable person. He wrote the book of Ecclesiastes, which is somewhat autobiographical. In this book Solomon, the golden child who the Lord had denied nothing admits his failings. "I said in my heart, 'Come now, I will test you with mirth; therefore enjoy pleasure';

but surely, this also was vanity. I said of laughter-'madness!'; and of mirth, 'what does this accomplish?' I searched in my heart how to gratify my flesh with wine, while guarding my heart with wisdom, and how to lay hold on folly, till I might see what was good for the sons of men to do under heaven all the days of their lives. I made my words great . . . ." ". . . and this was my reward from all my labor. Then I looked on all the works that my hands had done and on the labor in which I had toiled; and indeed all was vanity and grasping for the wind. There was no profit under the sun." " . . . Therefore I hated life because the work that was done under the sun was distressing to me, for all is vanity and grasping for the wind" (Ecc. 2).

By the end of his life Solomon was a wretched person. He confessed to hating life itself. He realized that he had blown it. All of his work would be destroyed. He knew that God would destroy the kingdom that he had built. It all had been a waste. He had spent his life on himself and had discovered the self-fulfilling prophecy of rebellion—destruction.

Solomon concludes the book of Ecclesiastes with words of a preacher pleading for those listening to him to take his advice. He says, "Let us hear the conclusion of the whole matter: Fear God and keep His commandments, For this is man's all. For God will bring every work into judgement, including every secret thing, whether good or evil" (Ecc. 12:13-14).

If you can take the word of anyone, take the final words of a dying man who blew one of the biggest opportunities for greatness in human history. Nothing except a broken heart and a destroyed life is to be gained from rebelling against God. Our rebellion, as in the case of Solomon's, will not only hurt us but will hurt those around us.

Solomon's acts of rebellion ultimately changed the future of the nation of Israel. God split the country. Solomon was to be the last human king of a united Israel. Things never were the same. To this day more than 3,000 years later, Israel has not recovered its former glory. According to biblical prophesy, it never will recover until the return of King Jesus himself.

Solomon says, "Remember now your Creator in the days of your youth" (Ecc. 12:1). If in our youth we decide to submit to the leadership and control of God, then He can guide us through all of the pitfalls of life. We can fulfill our purpose for living.

If we blindly believe that we are more capable of managing our lives than is the God who created us, then He will leave us alone. We truly can be "Master of our Domain." He has given us the will to make our own choices and the power to choose our own destiny. He warns us, however, where this will lead. The author of Romans clearly tells his readers, "The wages of sin is death."

Greater than the ability to chose one's own destiny is the ability to chose one's own Lord. If we are smart enough to realize we are not smart enough to choose our destiny, we will submit to Christ's leadership. "For the gift of God is eternal life through Jesus Christ our LORD." The secret is, "Whose Lord?"

Value 6

Becoming Divinely Beautiful

When my oldest daughter turned 2 and began to verbalize her thoughts, I asked her, "Anna, what do you want to be when you grow up?" She replied, "A bu-u-u-tiful pincess!" She wasn't concerned about being smart, strong, or funny. She wanted to be "bu-u-u-tiful!" Our second-born daughter was no different. Even from her earliest phrases emerged thoughts of beauty. I remember her saying things such as, "I wike my teacher. She's pwetty!" The first year she was old enough to understand about Christmas, I asked her what she wanted. She replied, "A bu-u-u-tiful dwess."

Why do all of us desire beauty from the time we begin to think coherently? Growing up I was the biggest tomboy God ever created. I could wrestle my brothers, race faster than their friends, and take them out with my toy gun. But when my door was closed, I remember staring in the full-length mirror and wondering if I, indeed, were beautiful. Sure that no one else in my family worried about such things, I was ashamed to admit that these thoughts even went through my mind. But I so-o-o wanted to be beautiful!

This is the way God made us. It is not flippant. It is not "unspiritual" or even unnatural. In fact, our ability to understand beauty is an expression of our spirit—the part of us that connects with God. God created beauty and put the pursuit of beauty deep within each one of us. God's love for beauty could not be more obvious than through a cursory observation of the world. Nature is nothing but all sorts of unique expressions of God's vision of beauty and glory. God created color and geometry. He created music and language. God put in the heart of humankind an understanding and appreciation of beauty in all of its forms. We can find it. Some of us can make it. All of us, however unrefined we think we are, enjoy it.

On a gut-honest, practical level, we have to admit that our own, personal, physical beauty is a chief concern for much of our lives.

In many ways our identity is directly tied to our physical appearance. It defines us and gives us our worth. We believe that being the most beautiful is important because we want to be the most special and the most important, at least to someone. Unfortunately for most of us, besides fighting an inner urge to be the most beautiful, we see and society confirms for us that beautiful people are more special and more important. Even when we are children, this is evident to us.

The ugly truth of the matter is that some people are more physically attractive than are others. This is disturbing. How does a good God who is supposed to love all people equally make our appearances less than equal? That isn't fair. Why is someone else prettier than I am? Or an even more cruel question: why do people with ugly character still sometimes seem to have been blessed with the most external beauty? In a just world, shouldn't the most godly and nicest people be the most physically beautiful?

Some eternal truths embedded in the Word of God shed light on this emotional turmoil. Obviously, a higher level of looking at beauty than just comparing facial features must exist. An unusual example springs from one of history's most fascinating men—a man I've already mentioned but who probably knew more about the subject of beauty than did any human ever to live: King Solomon.

The first and most important assignment given to King Solomon was the construction of God's temple. The construction of a house for God was something that his father, David, long had desired but had been forbidden by God Himself to build. Before David passed the kingdom over to his son, he instructed Solomon on the importance of this massive undertaking. God's temple was to be a place of unparalleled beauty. King David had spent years of his life collecting thousands of pounds of gold, silver, and precious gems for this project. Tens of thousands of master craftsmen had been assembled to create this singular and most amazing edifice. The Spirit of God himself guided David's hands as he wrote out word for word the design and layout of this beautiful place. How amazing to think that King Solomon had the unique privilege of building a monument of beauty designed by the Most High God! He was given word-by-word instructions on how to create God's vision of a beautiful architectural design: the perfect balance between understated elegance and glorious opulence.

However, beyond Solomon's professional interest in beauty, he probably is most well-known for his personal interest. In a previous chapter I've already referred to Solomon's lifelong fascination and collection of beautiful females—both wives and concubines. During his 40-year reign, he accumulated more than 700 trophy wives from all over the world. This was a man who understood beauty—especially female beauty. Over the course of his lifetime he did nothing but surround himself with beauty wherever he looked.

In Ecclesiastes 3:11, the book Solomon wrote at the end of his life, he makes a controversial observation about beauty. It is especially surprising because of his personal history. At this point in his life he has had time to mentally sort through a lifetime of women, estates, art, and gifts from all over the known world. After looking at it all, he makes a remarkable discovery about the nature of God: "He makes ALL things beautiful in His time." We could paraphrase that another way. All things that God makes are beautiful in His time. Every-thing that God makes is, indeed, beautiful or was made to be so. God's involvement in one's life creates beauty.

To live with a healthy self-image, one of the most important things for people to do is to accept and realize that when God made us, He created in each of us a unique image of beauty. We may not all be viewed as equally beautiful, but we are all indeed beloved beauties of an adoring Father-Creator. It sounds ridiculously simplistic, but it is nonetheless biblical and true. Everything God made—including every single one of us—is, by definition, beautiful.

One of the most powerful lies of Satan is to tell us that we are ugly. Rarely do I meet someone who does not think this about himself/herself, or at least did at one point in life. Of course I obviously am biased, but I consider my husband Jeff to be one of the most beautiful men on earth (he's not going to like me when he reads this!) One of the saddest stories I've ever heard him tell is about how he felt about himself during elementary and middle school. Little Jeff believed that he had the ugliest and most oversized nose ever designed. He honestly believed he was a real-life version of

Pinocchio—without the lies. He would go to school and then sit all day at his desk with his fingers cupped over his face. He didn't want anyone glancing around in class and seeing what he considered to be a grotesque disfigurement. He hated the way he looked. He would have done ANYTHING to change himself.

Jeff is not alone. Satan whispers destructive lies in our ears because he wants us to feel inferior and unworthy of love and respect. He wants us to loath ourselves. He tries to induce us to sell our dignity or our sexuality for less than what the masterpiece is worth. He does not want us to be able to recognize our value in Christ. He blinds us from recognizing our own true beauty and seeing the prizes we truly are.

Obviously most of us never will walk down runways or red carpets, but this does not make us unattractive. Society's vision of beauty shifts from generation to generation and is flakey at best. From my 21st-century perspective Mona Lisa doesn't seem even to be cute, much less to have a face that inspired a timeless portrait. To truly value yourself the way God does, recognize that each of us is a masterpiece conceived by God Himself. We are a work of art—an object of beauty in the sovereign eye of the Creator.

By definition objects of art are intrinsically unique. They are expressions of the Master Himself. Each of us is a true object of beauty. Each of us has things that unquestionably are distinctive and attractive. To feel pretty is not arrogance. Our beauty is not in the eye of the beholder; it is in the eye of the Creator. To see our own beauty is to observe fact, not hold to an opinion. Believe this deep within your heart.

Most of us have difficulty admiring our own selves. Stopping to look in the mirror and to even dare to smile and think, *I'm beautiful*, feels unnatural or conceited. Instead we look at the mole on the left side of our eye that seems to reach out and touch the mirror. We see nothing but an elephant-sized nose that dwarfs every other feature on our bodies. We see scars and protruding ears. We know every lump and bump from head to toe. We see only the things that bother us. We cannot be objective and even look for the beauty. Although it is there, we ignore it or don't appreciate it.

In a way self-loathing almost can feel spiritual or superior. We make ridiculous assumptions such as the one that says that women who don't wear jewelry or perfume are "above" superficial trends of fashion; a man who gets his unibrow waxed obviously has a masculinity problem; or my personal favorite—that exercise is only for people who are vain and have nothing to do. But ultimately pretending not to care about one's appearance is self-deluding and empty.

Instead of seeing only the ugly or pretending not to care one way or the other, by faith we must believe that God made each of us beautiful. Instead of defacing our bodies to hide an inferiority complex, make your appearance a matter of prayer. Just sit down and say, "Lord, show me what you made about me that is indeed beautiful. I believe in You, but I just don't see myself the way You do. I don't see why you made me like this. Who will find me attractive or special? When you look at me, Lord, what do you see?" Ask God to show you your own beauty. He will!

"He made all things beautiful in His time" are the words of the writer. To me the second part of this verse is as interesting as is the first. It implies what all of us already know to be true: all things are not beautiful all of the time. Beauty is not eternal. As a child I learned this difficult lesson. When I was in the first grade, two very disturbing things that affected the rest of my childhood happened to me. The first thing is that I was diagnosed as needing glasses. The second was that my mother got tired of fighting with me over my hair; she cut it over my ears.

In a few brief months I went from a relatively cute girl to a true, ugly duckling. I was a child of the '70s. So in typical '70s fashion, I found myself wearing huge, brown-rimmed glasses. I had a boy-cut around my ears. The kids at school called me "four-eyes." I hated the name. When I went out with my family, right in front of me, people often referred to the Akins' "three boys." My mother corrected them and informed them that I, indeed, was a girl, but the damage already was done.

For a long time I felt truly ugly. I felt ugly because, unfortunately, I was not at my most attractive stage. To this day my brother teases me about my "ugly phase."

Yet, even as a child I knew I wasn't as ugly as I felt. At night I would look in the mirror without my glasses and know I had more to me than could be seen through the brown rims. So that no one could see my haircut, I would wear baseball caps or a cute, red "Laura Ingalls" bonnet my parents had bought in Chattanooga, TN. If I weren't wearing my glasses and if I were in a hat, I believed that I actually looked like a girl—a frontier girl—like Laura in *Little House on the Prairie.*

Recently I spoke in a church in a small little village in northeast Brazil. During the break a woman talked to me about the people of her town. Brazilians, as a general rule, have very exotic beauty featuring dark eyes, light-brown skin, and thick, black hair. In this particular village somehow the conversation turned to some of the remarkable village children who ran around the church. As we talked, the woman nodded her head. Then she made a very interesting comment. "Yes," she remarked. "They truly are beautiful. Really there are no such things in the world as beautiful and ugly people. There are just rich and poor people." I didn't quite understand what she meant; she explained further. "The children all are beautiful, but as they grow up, things about them become problems that make them ugly: their eyes cross. We have no doctor," she explained. "We have no money for braces. No one wears sunscreen; their skin will turn to leather after a few short years." In other words, I understood her to say, "They all are beautiful now, but just wait to see what time will do to them."

If we buy into the lie that we are ugly, oftentimes we allow ourselves to believe that we can do nothing to help our plight. We choose to wallow in our own hideous self-pity. Perhaps we even feel holy all the while. I know people who are fat; instead of exercising progressively to work it off, they decide that nothing is to be done. Therefore they gorge all the more. I know others that think since they don't have the money to purchase expensive and designer clothing, they must despair and wear ratty T-shirts, stained blue jeans, and no deodorant.

Recognizing our own need to feel beautiful is important. We can identify the features and attributes that make up our own individual beauty and work to highlight these things. Nothing is holy about not wearing makeup or having no definable hair cut. Nothing is spiritual about wearing clothes that are out-of-date or that are unflattering. God cares about our self-image probably more than we do. He cares about our physical appearance. I have seen God miraculously provide money for His children to get braces, prescription eyeglasses, and even plastic surgery. Nothing is innately wrong with getting facial hair waxed, moles removed, or even a nose fixed. I believe that if God opens doors for his children to highlight special features of their appearance, he intends for them to walk through those doors. No shame exists in discreet primping.

Having totally endorsed those things that potentially lead us down the extreme road to selfish vanity, I encourage you to have a spiritual sense of balance. No health spas, diets, nor any amounts of injectable Botox have the power to create true beauty in a person. No matter what a person does or how much the individual spends, beauty that lies in our skin is really more of an illusion than a reality. At best it lasts no more than a few years and then is gone. It ultimately is not true.

True beauty is an indefinable essence that is timeless. It is a reflection of the Divine. Only one fundamental characteristic ultimately will define a beautiful person. This is the verse I earlier mentioned: "He makes all things beautiful in His time." The main lesson from this simple phrase that says so much is that the creator of beauty is God. God makes beauty; He takes TIME to do it. God takes time to make us beautiful because beauty is not, in its core essence, really about what we look like. It is about who we are, or rather who we are like.

The psalmist David—another fine curator of beauty—was the one that called this to my attention. For in the psalms, among his many descriptions of God the Father, is one attribute of God that David often describes as beautiful. It is the holiness of God. That struck me as odd. If we were to look in Roget's *Thesaurus* under the word beauty, the word "holy" would not even be included at the bottom of the list. Holiness, at least in the modern world, almost carries the opposite connotation. No one I know wants to be called "holier than thou." That's an insult. It certainly doesn't mean "more beautiful than thou." Holiness means perfection. It means something none of us ever can be. If God's holiness is anything, it's fearful—maybe even horrific. What, then, is so beautiful about holiness? What did King David see? Why would he say that?

Then I stop to think of people I believe to be beautiful. Who do I personally think is beautiful? Shockingly, it's really not the celebrities draped in Versacci and Prada, as glamorous as they are. The first person that springs to my mind immediately is my mother. To me she was one of the most beautiful people in the world. I have a picture of her behind the computer where I am writing these words. It was taken when I was 1 year old. It is one of my favorite pictures of her and always makes me smile.

In this photo my mother has beautiful, long brown hair, penetrating blue eyes, a perky nose, and high cheek bones. To me all those things are beautiful. But more is apparent to me as I gaze into her face. Her beauty is in her twinkling eyes. They reveal the tenderness of her heart. It's in her spunky smile that I so often saw growing up. So much of her beauty doesn't even emerge properly in a mere snapshot. Her beauty is so much deeper than the shape of her chin. It is in her personhood. Her beauty touches somewhere in my heart as I remember the countless picnics on which she took me, all the games of Uno we played, the hours she spent teaching me to ride a bike, to read, to cross-stitch, and to play the piano. Her beauty, although it has a physical element, is not fleshly or superficial. It is who she was that made her one of the most beautiful people in the entire world to me.

I also can reverse the logic to immediately identify some of the ugliest people I ever have known. One such guy was a drug addict who loitered the street where I lived as a teen-ager. His name was Kleber. Every day he would appear at our door and say, "Give me food!" He would yell at me in the harshest tone imaginable. I was extremely afraid of him, so I always gave him food, but I would slip it through the bars on our front door. After he finished eating, he'd look at me and say, "Give me something to drink." Once, when I told him no, he threw a fork at me. Another time I gave him lukewarm water; he threw the cup on the ground and shattered the glass everywhere. He was creepy. He always stank. He never smiled, but even if he could, he had broken teeth. He had rings and wrinkles all over his face. His drug-addicted existence clearly had taken a toll on his mind, soul, and somewhat decaying flesh.

Here's the point I see in David's observation: the more a person assimilates the character of God the Father, the more beautiful this person naturally becomes. Holiness creates beauty. An authentic smile creates beauty. A healthy and disciplined lifestyle creates beauty. A kind heart actually makes a person more beautiful. A physical element to this actually exists. Of course none of us ever can be perfectly holy. Only God is holy, but as we allow him to mold us into his likeness, our physical appearance actually will be affected in a positive way. We are not first and foremost flesh. Our physical appearance actually can change, depending on what is underneath the skin.

The Kleber saga dragged on and on all through my high school years. Every day Kleber stopped by the house. If I were there, he'd scare the jeepers out of me. I never understood why my mother endured this horrific man. Surely she could have called the cops or gotten rid of him somehow, but she put up with it. Kleber was a big man. He, to me, was a dangerous man. He was drugged out and wasn't in his right mind. I was convinced he was capable of snapping like I'd seen him do with that glass of water. My mother, however, was not scared of Kleber. Through my high-school days she humored this madman. When I left for college, he still was stopping by the house. Somehow, she saw whatever spark of humanity still was within his scarred body.

One day when Dad was home, Mom said, "Kleber, today you're going to take a bath." Somehow, she and my father wrestled a fully clothed Kleber into the shower. As they turned on the water, my father remembers Kleber screaming, "Why are you killing me?" He seemed to have no idea of what a shower was.

After he got cleaned up, they put some of my father's clothes on him. Then my father sat down and told him about Jesus. Soon after that, Kleber decided to give his heart to Jesus Christ. To make a long and complicated story short he eventually checked himself into a drug rehabilitation center and began the lifelong struggle of staying clean.

One summer, when I was home from college, my parents told me what had happened to Kleber. The drug rehabilitation center was run by a friend of my father's, so one day we went to visit. Kleber had been someone whom I had seen almost every day for four years. I knew what he looked like. I actually still can recall his putrid smell. But that day I was shocked at my re-encounter with Kleber. I vividly remember walking in and scanning the lunchroom full of recovering drug addicts. I looked, but I could not find Kleber. As I turned back to my parents, Kleber stood up, walked over to us, and gave my parents a hug. Daddy turned to me and said, "Christy, say hello to Kleber." I stared at Kleber. For the life of me I could not recognize him. Nothing, absolutely nothing, about him was even a shadow of the Kleber I knew. His physical appearance was totally different. His countenance was happy. His hair was cut; he smelled like cologne. But beyond that countless other things had changed about his physical appearance.

The more a person becomes like Christ, the more beautiful he or she becomes. Our bodies are connected with our souls and spirits. As the Spirit of God purifies and cleanses our souls, our bodies are positively affected. And, to the contrary, the more sin becomes a matter of lifestyle, the uglier physically a person will become. Sin corrupts completely. The wages of sin is death, states the writer of Romans, and death is ugly. The ugliness of sin eventually takes its toll even on our physical flesh. Kleber is not an anomaly; he is an "Everyman."

"He makes all things beautiful in His time." Beauty is a true mystery. It springs from the heart of God, since God is the creator and bestower of beauty. It is not a zero-sum game. It is an art, not a sport. It is not competitive. One person's beauty in no way detracts from another. My husband and I love Impressionistic paintings. One of our favorite painters is the great Claude Monet. Whenever we go to any significant art gallery, we always look to see if the gallery has a piece by this master artist. We appreciate his work because we find his style beautiful. I never have seen exhibited anything Monet created that I did not find amazing. Every piece is unique but yet similar enough to each other that I can see Monet in each one. All have value—in fact, so much value that I never will get closer to one than looking at it in a museum.

In the same way we are masterpiece creations of the same Supreme Artist. We can learn to appreciate things about us that are beautiful and enhance those as the Lord guides us. We also can seek to continually identify and treasure what is beautiful in other people—recognizing that ultimately my beauty is not significantly greater or lesser than that of any other person. Neither of us is more or less important. We all are reflections of the Master Creator.

Who I arbitrarily determine to be more beautiful in no way affects anyone's value, just as my preference for one Monet painting over another changes nothing about its ultimate worth. I am priceless because I am an expression of my Maker and because my Maker is a true genius. I can appreciate what is beautiful in others for the same reason. I can know that what is unique about them does not threaten me. We all are valuable because each of us is an individual and a beautiful realization of our Maker's vision.

However, in a true understanding of the fundamental nature of beauty, understand that the purest expression of our Creator's beauty is not about physical appearances at all. Beauty in all of its forms really is nothing more than a true reflection of God the Father. And a true reflection of our Lord Jesus Christ lies within the hearts of every one of us. As we grow in the Lord and in His holiness, we discover deeper beauty: a beauty that will not fade but that instead will grow with age. As we pursue a life of holiness and proximity to God our Father, we will become more and more beautiful. This is a beauty we will take with us to eternity. The closing words of the book of Proverbs say, "Charm is deceptive, and beauty is fleeting; but a woman who fears the Lord is to be praised." Such a woman will be praised because she truly is the possessor of divine beauty.

Value 7 (Part 1)

Understanding Money

"I Want Money, Lots and Lots of Money!" During his senior year in high school my husband campaigned heavily for this song to be the Senior Class graduation theme song. Stuffy students and horrified teachers quickly shot down this "absurd" idea. "How disrespectful!" they scoffed. Granted, Jeff's devious nature enjoyed the rise he got from his suggestion, but in a very real way, he actually personified the hopes and dreams of his graduating class. The Class of 1990 is not unique. Since 670 B.C. when the Turks invented money, we all want it—and in ample amounts.

We have a very good reason to want money. Practically speaking money means freedom. If I have money, I can do whatever I want. I can afford to buy; people will look up to me for my things. If I have enough money, I don't have to do the chores that make me miserable or slow me down. If I have money, I get to tell others what to do; they have to obey me. If I have money, I have access; my opinion matters. In a nutshell, if I have money, then I am an important person. If I do not, then I have little value. It can boil down to something no more complicated than a simple mathematical proportion.

If this is true, and most people in the world believe it is, then we need an answer to an important question about God. Why doesn't God make all people equally wealthy? Or, we could ask, why doesn't He make all people that are equally willing to work equally wealthy? Or we could ask, why doesn't He make all people of equal intelligence equally wealthy? Or, why doesn't He make all people of equal virtue equally wealthy? Or, why doesn't He make equally generous people equally wealthy? Perhaps I can admit that in looking at how God allows our world to function, He obviously has a totally different perspective on money. And, to be honest, that perspective doesn't make sense or seem fair.

Because wealth is intrinsically relative, it becomes a spiritually complicated issue. I am writing this in my house that sits on a cobblestone street in northeast Brazil. Two blocks down from my house is a slum. Every day children from this slum visit my house to ask for food. To be honest, after six years, many days I find this a nuisance. The kids ring my doorbell about 10 times in a row and ask, "Auntie, can I have a snack?" Sometimes, if they see me walking down the road, they actually will follow me for four or five blocks and even help me carry my bags just to get a snack. Sometimes, I wish they just would go away. Most already are dabbling with drugs. They pass the days begging at traffic lights and looking for pockets to pick. Inevitably I always end up giving them food.

One day I asked one of the children as he followed me out the door and down the block, "Sweetheart, why do you ask me for food?" He replied to me, "My house doesn't have food. I don't have a mother. My grandmother tells me to go out and get my own stuff." The child was only 8 years old. Sadly, hundreds of children just two blocks from where I live are in this situation.

Less than a year after having this conversation, our family returned to the States for our missionary "furlough." During our visit in the States, we watched a lot of news and really tried to catch up with what had gone on in America during our absence. I never will forget one television news magazine featuring poverty in America. In this particular piece the journalist went through an American slum and talked with victims of poverty. The report intentionally was designed to be a tear-jerker. I never will forget one of the journalist's acute observations. He accurately identified that one of the major problems in American slums is obesity. Residents of slums typically can't afford lean food. Neither do they have the education to understand proper nutrition. So unfortunately most of the food stamps and/or available money are spent on cheap, processed, empty foods such as chips and cookies.

What a stark contrast! In America slums are identified because the children are obese. In Brazil slums are places in which children are desperately thin and spend their days running from house to house begging for food.

The truth is, in a relative sense, Brazil also is a wealthy country. When I was in high school, my parents moved us to Zimbabwe, Africa. Being a bored teen-ager, I volunteered at an African daycare center at the seminary at which my parents taught. The experience stayed with me. At lunch time the teachers lined up all the children. We passed out little bowls. The children would go to the first worker; she would put into the bowl a large spoonful of mush (a corn-meal-and-water paste). Then the children would go to the next, who would dish out one little brown bean and place this on top of the mush. She then would scoop out a little bean water and pour it on the remainder of the mush in order to flavor this dish. I then watched these children sit down in the dirt outside the serving area and lick their little bowls clean. I watched in silence. Not one child complained about such a miserable meal. The noises emerging from their mouths were just like noises from any of the kids I have served sodas and pizza in other parts of the world. These children did not view themselves as deprived. They were being fed. In Zimbabwe poverty is defined a different way. Here are many, many children who would love to have the opportunity to stand in line to receive corn mush and one solitary bean. They would dream of a day in which they could run from house to house begging for bread. They would love to do this because in their country, they can run around all day long and not find anyone who has any food to give them. Their country is in a perpetual state of famine.

From just a cursory glance around the globe, one can see that God's perspective of poverty and wealth is different from our own. His goal is not to enrich every person on this earth. He created heaven for that. He views earth as a passing place in which, through a series of life events, we learn to love and know God in preparation for the wealth that He has prepared for us in heaven. For God money does NOT mean freedom. Christ means freedom. For God money does not mean importance. Our value is grounded in the fact that we are created in the image of an almighty God.

John 3 clearly states the truth that God indeed does love the entire world. However, all over the world, primarily but not solely because of humanity's sin, people live in poverty and hunger. Even if we are not totally financially destitute, most of us believe that we are not as financially well-off as we want or should be. This is not something new to the 21st century. This has been true since the days of Genesis.

God's sovereign will clearly is not to starve people, but He doesn't seem to feel obliged to accept the responsibility of financing a world that is in constant rejection of Him and His plans. In fact, financial prosperity is not even in the cards for some of His most faithful servants.

This brings up the obvious question about believers in Him. Is God just going to abandon to the fates of the world those that have entrusted their lives to His care? Must they suck it up and stick it out until death takes them to heaven? That sounds horrible! The answer is most emphatically NO! God is deeply aware of every individual situation. He knows and cares deeply for the specific circumstances of every true believer. He watches out for each of us in spite of whatever chaotic mess we may have found ourselves in along the way. King David gives a powerful testimony of God's faithfulness to His people when he writes in Psalm 37:25 that he never has seen His seed begging bread. In the entire time that David lived, he never saw someone go hungry if that person truly trusted God. I only can imagine how hunger prevailed during those days when people tilled the earth from season to season and hoped to gather enough grain to survive.

Whatever happened amazed King David enough to write a worship poem to praise God for it. I personally am amazed on those occasions when I have been allowed to see up-close God's miraculous providence. God truly does provide for those who trust in Him.

During our fourth year on missionary assignment in Brazil, my husband and I, together with our two young associates, held a year-long discipleship campaign all over our state. We used Henry Blackaby's best-selling workbook entitled *Experiencing God*. One of my absolute favorite moments in teaching *Experiencing God* occurred in week three of the course when I, as the teacher, began the lesson by asking the age-old, existential question, "How do you know that God is really real?"

Being a Western-minded logic-driven person I expected to hear my students spurt out logically thought-out answers that apologetically proved in their minds the existence of God. However, not one of my students ever answered this question that way. In fact, in every group, I was shocked and overwhelmed by the stories I heard. One student related that one day she was completely out of food. She had no food, no money, and no job. She recently had accepted Christ into her heart and so had decided to give Him this problem. She said, "Lord, I have no food. I have given my heart to you. What do you want me to do?" Since she was new in her faith, a part of her expected God to speak to her audibly. For a few minutes she sat at her barren kitchen table before she felt foolish. Finally realizing that nothing was happening, she got up and set about doing her usual housework. She opened her front door to sweep out some dirt when she looked down and spotted a basketful of food on her doorstep. To this day she never has learned who put that food there. Everyone she knew denied knowing anything about it.

I remember another man, with his eyes full of tears, recounting a similar tale. He was the father of two small children. Samuel had been laid off work and had completely run through all of his resources. He said he remembers heartbrokenly leaving the house in the morning because he had no bread to leave his children for their breakfast. He did not know how he could face them, since he knew they would be hungry. He felt totally to blame. He believed he was a failure as a father and a husband. Just as he left for another day of job hunting, a neighbor stopped by and asked if she could drop off some bread and butter. Somehow, in confusion, both husband and wife had gone to the bakery that morning for breakfast. The food was going to waste, she said. She thought she'd just drop it off to see if they could use it. It was a miracle, he told me. Such a thing never had happened before and never has happened since. That day he found a job.

Living in the Third World, I have had the privilege of hearing hundreds of miraculous stories from people seemingly forgotten in the middle of nowhere and living literally on the brink of death. I heard a pastor tell how he was locked in a freezer on a merchant ship. God miraculously blew the door open and spared his life. I heard a woman tell about a time she was riding down the highway on top of a big delivery truck and was trying to catch a ride into the big city. She began to fall off the truck. She yelled, but the driver was inside the cab and could not hear her. She knew she was falling off until suddenly she felt a hand push her back on top. This spared her life. Thousands and thousands of unrecorded miracles occur all over the world. None of them ever will be told or recorded for posterity. They are not statements God is making to prove His existence to the skeptics. They are not showy miracles for a TV audience. They merely are the acts of a loving Father Who is very interested and serious about feeding and protecting His own. God is in the business of taking care of His children.

But God's interest in money goes way beyond just feeding people. That is just the beginning. The Bible seems very clear that our resources are gifts from the Lord. He requires that his children take very seriously the stewardship of these resources. Proverbs 3 is almost entirely devoted to this subject as it directs a person seeking a godly wife. God advises men not to marry women who are flippant about money. Nothing is flippant about the subject. Jesus talked about it throughout His sermons. Several parables deal specifically with treasure or money. Back then money was a primary concern as it continues to be today. Money is serious. Money is important. But wealth is not everything.

The Bible is consistent in its attitude toward money. In the Bible money is treated as a vehicle—not as a passion. Never in either the Old or New Testament do we see God endorsing a life dedicated to the pursuit of wealth. We are to pursue God and a deeper relationship with Him. He is the object of our passion. Money in no way means God's blessing. It does not mean a superior position in God's kingdom. It simply is a vehicle that He will use in different ways in our lives. God has a specific plan for each of our lives. Obviously money plays a role; it is not the centerpiece.

Not long after I arrived in Brazil, I visited a church called the "Universal Church." At the time it was a new cult group in Brazil and seemed to be taking off like no cult ever had in the past. Its churches were packed and had services all day, every day—totally unbelievable. My Portuguese tutor and I were interested in this phenomenon and, as a field trip, decided to attend one of its services. We were assured the services would last only one hour. The building was beautiful. We sat in movie-theater type seats instead of traditional church pews. The uniformed ushers wore ties. It reminded me of a symphony. Behind the pulpit was a partially constructed, golden-colored wall where members could purchase blocks for the building of God's Kingdom. The service we attended started punctually at 11 a.m. on a Friday. After the initial prayer the first thing the preacher did was tell us about the problems of the world and how Christ could fix these problems. Then he held an offering. After the first offering he led a prayer in which we could receive a special blessing from the Lord if we contributed financially to the Kingdom of God. He then asked us to approach the front and give God our "all." This obviously involved cash. My tutor and I were the only ones in the congregation who did not go forward to receive "God's blessing."

He then asked whether any demons were present and directed them to approach the front. Two men supposedly possessed by demons went to the front. These demons were cast out. People who at that time needed the Lord's power as displayed by the casting-out of the demons were instructed to raise their hands and prepare for an offering. My tutor and I were the only ones with our arms not in the air to receive the Lord's power. As a direct result of our failure to comply, three uniformed women with oil approached us. They put oil on our foreheads and laid their hands on our heads. They then prayed to God and asked Him to remove from our bodies the demons that kept us from giving our lives to God. After this prayer the minister had a fourth offering in which we were given one final opportunity to rectify our sins before the Lord.

At this point in the service I felt so much pressure to give money that I almost did just to keep people's condemning eyes from glaring into the back of my head. I felt as though I were a sinner. Everyone seemed to be staring. The minister's eyes bore into us as he gave his altar call. Finally, the service ended. The women who had put oil on our foreheads turned to us and smiled. It was over; we were free to go home.

This personifies a complete and total lack of understanding of God's relationship with money. Avoid making money the centerpiece of your life. Certainly avoid making money the centerpiece of any church. God does not want His people begging. He doesn't want them begging for bread. He definitely doesn't want His church or any pastor turning Him into a beggar.

God doesn't associate His blessing with the amount of money we are willing to give to a specific cause. God made gold, petroleum, minks, and diamonds. He could make our decorated paper if He found doing so necessary! He is our Heavenly Father. What father would submit His children to such treatment? What father begs His children for whatever pittance they have saved up in their piggy banks? If a child of God needs something, he or she can ask it of the Lord and see what He provides. He may supply it through a gift. He may supply it through a job. He may make us wait. He may help us reevaluate our "need." He may want us to evaluate how we've used the resources He's already given us. If God needs something, He has all the resources in the world to provide it. Never trust anyone who resorts to begging in God's name or begging for God. Never allow yourself to be reduced to such a state. Such a state is not of God. If you find yourself in such a position, evaluate what's wrong. You'll find a fundamental error in how you are administering the resources God already has given you.

Money is a vehicle of God—a vehicle God wants us to administrate effectively and gain honorably. Through the parable of the talents (Matt. 25:14-30) Jesus drives this point home. In this story, a businessman goes away and divides resources unequally between his three servants. When he returns, he rewards the ones who used what he gave him most effectively. He tears into the lazy person who did nothing with his opportunity.

After college my husband and I really had no idea what we would do with our lives. All through high school I had wanted to be a lawyer and a diplomat. With the idea of getting married and having kids, all of that was being called into question. My husband always had dreamed of being a famous international journalist, but after four years of journalism in an unknown school far away from any significant news center, he realized that immediate job prospects were a challenge. He would have to derive a unique plan. We prayerfully began looking at all kinds of different options and career paths. One such path occurred through an obscure door. One of our favorite college professors knew a man in Japan who had written our university and offered to host two graduates looking for work. At that time Jeff and I knew nothing about Japan or Japanese culture, but this man went on to discuss the financial prospects. This got our attention. He claimed that a conversational English teacher in Japan could receive anywhere from $20 to $50 per HOUR! His company was preparing to hire two new teachers. He would be more than happy to help the newcomers make the transition.

After counting our coins, Jeff and I decided that we had no better career option than to spend what little money we had in savings on two tickets bound for Nagoya, Japan. Perhaps after a year in the Orient, we would know what to do with our lives. Our families and friends thought we had lost our minds. I still remember sitting in the Los Angeles airport and looking around the gate. I saw a man in the corner practicing karate as he watched his own movements reflected in the window. It seemed so bizarre. People were eating rice rolled up in green wrapping paper (at least that's how I saw it). The titles on the magazines were vertical. It all looked odd. Jeff and I really had felt God's leadership in this decision. We wanted to go. We were excited. But at that moment I felt totally foreign and wondered what God was doing with my life.

To make a very long and complex story short, after a rough start, the kind man helped us secure jobs. We moved to a quaint Japanese town at the foot of Mt. Fuji and spent 13 months there teaching English to businesspeople. I never would have imagined God providing for us in that way, but we were able to stash away some cash. Through our savings that year, we were able to return to the States and establish ourselves debt-free in what has turned out to be a career so far as missionaries. Obviously we never have been rich. But we always have enjoyed relative financial stability. Jeff and I have disagreed and argued about a lot of things. But we never have fought about money. This is certainly not because we're spiritual. But amid our myriad of newlywed mistakes, we did do one thing right. From the very beginning of our marriage we decided to obey and follow the Lord's lead in determining our finances.

This is the point. When people give their lives to Jesus Christ, they give ALL of their lives to Jesus. That means that their futures no longer are their own. Their careers no longer are their own. Their money no longer is their own. If I am a follower of Christ, everything in my pocket or bank account already belongs to God—not just the commonly misconstrued 10 percent. I have a plan in how money will get into my pocketbook. He has a plan on how to use it.

Whether or not we honor God with our finances and allow Him to manage it, ultimately it is His. If only we could just rest in that, we could relax. God understands money! He wants to guide us to becoming ingenious with the resources that He has given us. He wants to make the money that He has given us work FOR us. He knows the source of our money. He has a plan for every dollar that He puts into our care. He knows how to make it grow. He doesn't want us to gamble or waste away our earnings. Neither does He want us to live a Spartan existence eating leaves, wearing brown robes, and giving all of our money to one cause or another. Instead He wants to teach us how to carefully use and invest money for His glory. He wants us to live in a way that brings honor to Him and is a blessing to the many people we meet.

Money is a vehicle that God intends for us to learn how to use effectively because it will make us stronger. Proverbs 31 says of a godly wife, "She considers a field and buys it; from her profits she plants a vineyard. She girds herself with strength, and strengthens her arms." Money often will be a vehicle that He uses to protect us and make us a blessing in the lives of others. Money is serious. Although God consistently blesses His children with nice things, outings, trips, and even collectibles, we can realize that the object of our money is not to shamelessly indulge, pamper ourselves, or impress others. God gives it a much greater purpose—to serve and honor the Lord.

We become stronger the more effectively we use our money. We become more effective with money the more we truly can see its purpose and are not controlled by the incredible urge to spend. When money is concerned, most of us think of ourselves primarily as consumers. We think the purpose of money obviously is to spend—to buy stuff we want or need. We think being smart means knowing how to stretch it. People who are savvy are those that clip coupons, go to yard sales, and sniff out bargains. They are those who buy more stuff for less money. Although being an astute consumer is admirable, the biblical principle is much greater.

As playwright Oscar Wilde would say, understanding the cost of something versus its actual worth is important. Some things are worthless, no matter what they cost. Other things are precious and priceless. Some things we perceive as essential are no more than con jobs pulled off by marketers. Determining cost and value can be incredibly complex. This also is a spiritual issue that God teaches us through time.

Allowing God to teach us how to use money wisely is a discipline that must start at as early an age as possible and must continue throughout one's entire life. Many aspects and gazoodles of pitholes are out there when money is concerned. On the street I met an old woman who shells cashew nuts for a living. My neighbor who introduced me told me that the man who buys her cashews lies to her and cheats her when he calculates her payments. She is too ignorant to know the difference. She needs help. But we all do . Although some of us have more sophisticated circumstances than did the cashew sheller, we all are vulnerable.

On the other hand many opportunities as well as places for help and advice exist. God brought my neighbor into the life of this old woman to help her understand her finances and save her from exploitation. If we are open to allowing Him to instruct, He ingenuously helps each of us.

All people—no matter their age, gender, or earning potential—can make a lifelong habit out of understanding their finances and working honestly to build wealth. Math and money are not everyone's fortes, but they are everyone's concern. Only one person cares more about our financial security than we do. That is the Lord. Being careful and prayerful about money is like being careful and opened-eared to a boxing trainer during a boxing match. We don't want to listen to his advice, but when we choose to ignore it, we usually end up flat on our backs and in a lot of pain.

Most single people I know plan to get married some day. If we are not prepared, money will cause major marital conflict and even divorce. In many homes the woman will be the administrator of the home. This role is not demeaning or "constraining." Actually Proverbs 31 seems to view the model, godly woman as her family's primary caregiver or administrator. But what does that term mean?

To some, *home administrator* translates into some '50s stereotype of baking cookies, mopping floors, breeding babies, and sewing patches. But the *Leave It To Beaver* model really is not biblical. In fact, for all of human history, being a wife and mother never has meant what we see on *Nick at Night*.

Abigail Adams is one of my true heroes of womanhood. She was a godly woman, a successful wife, mother, and First Lady of the United States of America. Her major role in life was that of a homemaker, but look what that entailed for her! She married a lawyer who owned Braintree—the family plantation. Even at the beginning of John Adams' law career, he spent much of his time away in the city. Abby addressed all the day-to-day crises in the house and on the grounds. Her lot became that of supervising the farm in his absence. After the first shots were fired in Boston, John Adams became a revolutionary and was gone for years. Abigail's role expanded even more. With little help and on wartime rations she successfully ran the farm. She managed the finances. Abigail reared her five kids. Even though she herself had had no formal education, she was forced to Homeschool all of them, one of whom grew up to be the fourth President of the United States. She did these things because she took very seriously her job as home administrator. This entailed managing her children, her house, and what is most overshadowed—their property and resources.

Managing a household means being responsible for life. In any marriage, someone will have to take the lead in selecting the family house, purchasing most of the things a family will own, paying the bills, managing the mortgage, budgeting weekly expenses, and planning and saving for vacations, along with the gazillion other financial details of running the household on a daily basis. Women often are the ones to do this. Even if they work outside the home, they often are more attuned to intricate details of their home and the needs of their children. That's why wives, as well as husbands, benefit from learning the task of money management God's way.

God has put more thought into our financial well-being than we have. He has a plan for our lives. He knows the resources we need to fulfill His purpose. He puts us in family units or teams and teaches us to use the vehicle of money more effectively and productively in building the future He has designed for us. I have immense freedom in knowing that the limit on my credit card in no way correlates to my worth in the world and before God. My life has purpose and meaning if I live it by God's design. This may or may not involve a large paycheck for me. Freedom is to live free from the pressure to acquire and to trust God to lead us to financial stability. It is living with the understanding that money is God's vehicle just as our brains or our bodies are. In the Master's hands it is an instrument of peace and a blessing.

Value 7 (Part 2)

Pursuing Economy

Jeff had asked me to marry him; a good friend's parents were celebrating our engagement by taking us to eat at the Spaghetti Warehouse. This particular couple in my mind was the portrait of "red-state" America. He works in insurance. She is in education. They have two children—a boy and a girl—and are active members of a local church and other social organizations.

During our four years in college, we had developed a special relationship with this couple. The outing was a highlight. After we ordered, we began the excited chatter about our upcoming wedding mingled with the latest gossip from the college campus. Nothing spectacular happened during dinner.

I probably would barely remember the meal except for a comment made about midway through the main course. In a lighthearted effort to warn Jeff of the upcoming hazards of marriage and in typical husbandly fashion, the husband took a gentle stab at his wife. He complained that she had been forced to take a second job at the mall to support her extravagant spending habits. She, of course, denied the allegation. It was not the spending that was out of the ordinary. It was just the income that was short.

The lighthearted banter continued until the husband, in an effort to prove his case, proceeded to showcase his wife's brand-new purse sitting under the table. It was a designer purse that had cost well over the monthly income of a middle-class family in most developing nations. He went on to expound how no sane person ever would pay that much for a bag designed solely to drag around and stash under restaurant tables. She rolled her eyes, leaned over to me, and whispered loudly enough for everyone to hear, "He just doesn't understand that a purse is not an expense. It is an investment." Of course nothing else was made of the matter; the conversation moved on. But I really began to think about what she said. At that time I was working on campus part-time making five dollars an hour. That purse would cost me weeks of labor at my current rate. Was a designer purse an extravagance or an investment? This couple obviously disagreed on the answer. Even though they were joking, I could tell that in this family, finances were not always a laughing matter.

Behind the glittering department-store windows and magazine ads live questions that cause anxiety and even sadness. How does a godly person spend money? Is a godly person frugal like Ben Franklin's "Old Richard"? Is having nice things sinful? Do I give all my money away to the poor? Is caring about fashion or designers wrong? Do I hide any money I have so people think I'm poor? What things constitute investments? What things constitute "wastes of money?" How does one ever know the difference? The bottom line is: How can I decide how to spend my money in a way that is wise? How can I control it and not have it control me?

Many good books by godly individuals give specific and detailed instructions on how to balance spending in every area of life. As I said before, a wise person seeks instruction and becomes a lifelong student of good finances. However, my parents passed down several simple rules of thumb. These are easy principles to memorize. All my life I have tried to follow them. My husband, although born a thousand miles away from where I was, was reared on these same principles. These are biblical. They apply to every generation, every culture, and every economic group. If followed properly they actually will make you live longer, healthier, and for sure happier. And if you so choose, they could help you get married and stay married.

Principle 1—NEVER, NEVER, NEVER SPEND WHAT YOU DON'T HAVE

People have been doing this since the days of Moses and the Old Testament prophets. The Old Testament is stocked full of warnings about debt. This involves the dangerous idea of spending money that I plan on making in the future when things are better than they are now. It is a pit many well-meaning people find practically impossible to avoid. We blame the credit-card companies for their entrapment and exorbitant interest rates. We blame television and the intoxicating commercialism. We blame the clock and our inability to control our time. The list goes on and on and on.

No matter how long we live, this world will find more things that we need to buy than most of us have money to spend. It's bigger than capitalism. It's more powerful than the free-market. Maybe it is greed. Maybe it's our instinctive drive to progress. Whatever the reason, things to buy always abound! All the power and might of history's most powerful governments can't even control it. At the time of this writing, the U.S. Government actually owes $7,822,412,473,812.72, with an estimated increase of 1.64 billion dollars added to this total per day.

The drive to spend is a powerful force. But before you spend all of your future earnings, decide what is actually worth having and what you can do without. I relearn this lesson every time I visit my mamaw and papaw in the foothills of northeast Tennessee.

My grandparents still live on the same small farm on which my mother was reared. For my entire life they have had the same furniture, down to a 100-year-old pump organ that sits in their basement. I can smell furniture polish and bleach as I look at my mamaw's sewing machine and my papaw's shop. The fresh smells make my mind drift off to the past and the happy history contained in each item of their home. When I sit on their porch and eat cucumbers straight from the garden, I can envision a much simpler life. They never made house payments on their house. They built it themselves. They hardly buy groceries. How could you when you've eaten nothing but home-grown produce all your life? They do have air-conditioning, but they run it only when they need it. They have a clothesline on which they hung clothes for years. They don't have cable. Their rotary phones still are in perfect working order. They have a freezer full of meat from a cow my uncle butchered. Everything feels simple. Everything feels sturdy. Everything always makes more sense to me there.

Two years before my mother died, my mamaw's church made a decision to travel to Brazil and build a church building for the people of a small community in the vast and primitive Brazilian interior. Mamaw's church is a small church with no more than 120 members. All are residents of a small rural community. None really can afford extravagant trips abroad, but they believed in the cause. So, in good Tennessee Volunteer fashion, this church decided to spend the six months before the trip raising the cash. My mamaw was on the "apple-butter-and-breakfast committee." No one could count how many jars of apple butter she made that year or how many eggs she scrambled on Saturday mornings. Community dwellers—members of the church or not—would arrive at the church for breakfast, fellowship, and to support the cause. That little church raised more than $30,000 for its trip. Members traveled without a cent of debt. After that initial project these members have traveled to Brazil many more times and felt excitement many people find only on movie screens.

Debt is something most people incur because, for the most part, we believe we "deserve" certain things. Jillions of times I have heard people say, "OH, what the heck, I'll just charge it. I deserve this!" Great irony seems to exist in this statement. It's true, but not in the spirit in which this statement usually is spoken. If we are dumb enough to create needless debt, most of the time we deserve the consequences.

Another restaurant, another outfit, another hair color, another movie, or another opportunity always are available. Another sale, another bargain, another discount, another project, another investment always is around the next corner. The people pushing these things are professionals. Their jobs are to stick their hands in our pockets. Society doesn't take long to commit every cent in our present and future possession.

One of the greatest scams with which I personally have been involved was with a sleek investment advisor. Presenting a no-risk, fail-safe plan, he talked my husband and me into letting him manage our money while we were overseas. We thought that this arrangement was perfect and this man had discovered the secret to moving the world. Everything was going to plan until one fateful day in 2000. This was sometime after the stock market had begun to plummet under the weight of the deaths of the dot-coms. Bedrock American companies such as Enron, Tyco, WorldCom, and Arthur Andersen were being paraded into courtrooms all over America. Millions of lives were being wrecked by financial corruption deep within corporate America. We watched with interest, but basically these were just news reports on television until we got a phone call during our vacation in Arkansas. We had traveled there to visit Jeff's family and to introduce them to our brand-new, baby girl—Elizabeth Christine—who had been born in South America.

"I'm sorry. All your money is gone. It's their fault; they won't let me fix it anymore," said our bereaved financial advisor over the phone. This made little sense to us. We immediately were outraged, called my parents—who also had placed their money in his care—and got in our car and drove an hour and a half to speak face-to-face with this big, bad institution.

When we got there, we met his boss. The kind man apologized. We were not the only ones. The man told us that not only had we lost all of our money, but we actually were $250,000 in debt. My father owed more than $500,000. It was a sum we never could pay back. Our investment advisor had borrowed money in our name to invest in fail-safe projects. The problem was, he concealed it. For months, he had kept borrowing and borrowing larger sums because he knew things were going to change. No one would be the wiser after the markets bounced back and he paid everyone back.

Needless to say, years later, the markets have yet to bounce back completely. He got caught. His strategy was a total disaster for everyone involved—his embarrassed investment company, us, and of course, the misguided advisor himself. Lawyers got involved to help us recover some of our money and to clear our names from this insurmountable debt. It was personally humiliating; the financial devastation was terrible for everyone.

For all of his fancy training, this investment broker would have been much better off had he just applied the basic biblical rule, "Never spend what you don't have." Don't borrow money—even if this means passing up the opportunity of a lifetime! Proverbs 22:7 says that the one who borrows becomes a servant to the lender. This always will be true. Borrowing money will rob you of personal freedom faster than will anything outside of drug use.

Now having stated the rule, like in English grammar, a few good and well-calculated exceptions do seem to exist—the financing of a home being the most obvious. A person must pay to live somewhere. Although, paying cash for a home might be nice, doing so usually is impossible. But even a loan on a home that will go up in value over time can still make you a slave if you are paying more monthly than you realistically can afford. It can still strap you and create extreme amounts of stress. Use prayerful wisdom.

The other possible exception could be a school loan. In most cases people can't afford to pay for school as they go. They must go to school in order to make money later in life, but they don't have any money to go to school. This, too, probably is more of an investment than real debt, but any loan is risky and dangerous. After college I briefly entertained the idea of getting my master's degree in education from Vanderbilt University, a school I admire very much. I visited the school and talked to the people in the education department. Soon after we returned from Japan, I was serious enough about it to discuss the situation with Jeff. He looked at me and laughed, "Why would you pay $60,000 for a job that's only worth $30,000 a year?" I hated to admit it, but he was right. My return, even for education, would not justify the high price tag. I ended up getting my master's from the University of Memphis for less than $5,000. Even if it is for school, a loan is a heavy and burdensome weight around the neck of its victims. It has the potential to suck life and joy from a normally happy person. And loans—even student ones—linger on for YEARS. Only borrow money for school if you have prayed through it carefully and believe God himself has authorized the loan. I have two wonderful friends who went to school with me. They graduated 11 years ago. One of the biggest regrets they have is their school loans. They want pretty furniture and a new car. They have children they want to take on vacation. They want to be a part of social and church projects around the world. They have dreams—all of which have been put on hold because their bills each month take every extra cent. They got their degrees but believe they overpaid for them by going to the wrong school for the type of career they were planning.

God has called his children to freedom! The quickest way to lose freedom is to incur debt. Debt is a prison that can keep people locked up for years. It gives normal people dark circles under their eyes and ugly lines all over their faces. It's a source of shame and humiliation. If God wants a person to attend college, He has a plan for how to pay for it. It may be junior college. It may be scholar-ships. It may be work-study. It actually could be student loans. But NEVER does God intend for his children to graduate from college with heavy burdens of bills they cannot repay.

Principle 2—SPEND DELIBERATELY AND SLOWLY

Impulse shopping is the goal of every grocer and sales clerk in the world. Milk is not accidentally always in the back of the store. Fifty-percent off items are not accidentally always hidden behind the onslaught of new arrivals. This is the reason why I hate to go to Wal-Mart or Target. I can enter a dime store to buy nothing more than toothpaste and leave with a bill totaling my weekly paycheck. All these things I purchased are stuff I found I "needed" once I was inside the shiny, beautiful store.

The opposite of impulse shopping is planned shopping. List-oriented people do this better than others do, but unless you have lots of money to blow, planned shopping is a much wiser strategy just as planned eating is better than impulse eating. It's a habit worth acquiring, even if it doesn't naturally occur, as it doesn't for me.

Planned shopping means simply to invest thought into what you want to buy somewhat specifically before you even leave your home. It means not buying anything you haven't thought about for at least a couple of days—including sales and including food. Every

Sunday night or Monday morning, I sit down with an index card and write out what I think will be the meals for our family for the week. My husband likes to order pizza every Wednesday night, so I put that on the agenda. We usually eat out for lunch on Sunday, so I put that on the index card as well. For us, since we have a limited budget and a family of four, we usually eat the rest of our meals at home. So, I write out what meals we plan to cook. I go to the pantry and fridge and see what I need to buy to make these dishes. Then, I sit down with another index card and write out what I need to buy. We drink lots of soft drinks, so I check our pantry. My husband eats Milky Ways and Hershey bars, so I check his deliciously decadent candy drawer as well. Then, one day in the week, I go to the store and purchase the things on my list. I may, by way of impulse, pick up a new dessert or something the store is promoting, but I do so consciously and reservedly. I do not run up a chaotic bill simply purchasing things we like to eat or happen to be without (which is how I first started out my career in food shopping). As we go through the week, we can change our plans or switch the meals, but we have some sort of structure and order in our eating. It keeps me away from the store. Regrettably for me, the more I go, the more I spend. It's unavoidable, so I have to plan!

This principle of planned eating actually could be applied to any kind of shopping. Although I don't know of anyone hyperorganized enough to list on an index card all their outfits for the week, my system could be applied to clothes. Fashion gurus tell us to go through our closets every so often and actually count how many outfits we have. Divide them into three categories: fancy, casual, or grungy. Although this never is a problem in the Third World, in some countries people have hundreds of combinations of clothes and still have nothing cute to wear on any given day of the week.

My husband, who is the polar opposite of what we call metrosexual, has never understood this problem. He pulls out a pullover and khakis for casual days, a tie for formal days, and shorts and a T-shirt for grungy days. He has three types of clothes for three types of occasions. He needs only about three changes of each. He goes shopping about twice a year and returns good to go.

I, however, on the other hand, always have struggled to find clothes. For years, I looked into my closet and saw only clothes that I hated. My shirts never matched my slacks. My dresses, which most of the time were outdated, didn't accentuate my assets. I only felt averagely dressed, even though I seemed to be spending lots of money on clothes and had a closet full of something.

After I was frustrated for years, my husband finally helped me get a grip on my problem. I had a shopping problem. I wasn't shopping purposefully; I wasn't buying stuff I liked. Together, we went through my closet and threw onto the bed everything I didn't like. I studied some fashion magazines and talked to some people who were more fashion-savvy than myself. Then Jeff and I went together and bought two work outfits in which I felt comfortable. Up to that point I always had shopped on the back racks (the half of the half of the half of the half mark-down racks); but Jeff said, "It's not a bargain if you don't like it and we end up throwing it on the bed." Together, that day, we bought one really cute outfit; I really liked it. I didn't buy more. I didn't add any bargains at the last minute that I happened to notice were on sale. I just bought the outfit I set out to purchase. For several years that outfit was one of my favorites.

As I stared at my bed and saw the clothes that I was rejecting, I began to wonder where I got all these items. At one time I must have liked them. I purchased almost every single one of them. Then, my spending pattern started to emerge in my mind. Most of my clothes were fall or winter. That is because my birthday is in October. I get most of my clothes money from gifts on my birthday or at Christmas. As soon as I got the money, I excitedly would rush out and buy new stuff. I would try to stretch out the cash as far as possible and get multiple outfits that, at the time, I seemed to like. But most of the time, I couldn't find many things that I really, really liked, so I ended up getting things that I just "kind-of" liked and hoped they would grow on me after I went home. I was buying just because I could or had available funding. Oftentimes, I would prudently wait until I could grab some bargains, but here again, I was making the same mistake. I was buying stuff as my resources became available and not to match a specific need.

This got me to thinking—how many outfits does a woman actually need? Do I need 10 work outfits and four church outfits? How many pairs of jeans do I need? How many pairs of shoes do I need? Of course I can't answer that question for anyone but myself, but I do think it's a question each of us must ask ourselves and not just about clothes. How much is enough? Most of us actually do have limited resources. We cannot just go out and buy new things for every day of the week. Even if we did have the money to do so, that probably would not honor God. So, here's a simple strategy: get your birthday money, Christmas money, or whatever budget money you plan on allocating to clothes. Set it aside. Then purchase clothes systematically instead of impulsively. Buy maybe one new outfit every month or six weeks. Choose between fancy, casual, or grunge as the needs change. Buy the accessories for a specific outfit you are building, not just because they're cute. Never buy more than one outfit at a time. Hold out for the next go-around. Remember that something else always is out there to buy. Never buy something ONLY because it's a bargain. Five dollars is a donation to the store if you purchase something you will wear only once. Never buy something if you have doubts about it. If you have to stare at the mirror, turn around and around, and scrunch your nose, it's not worth buying. However much you like something in the store, you will like it less and less (except for jeans) as time goes on. Clothes, like cars, depreciate immediately as you drive away from the lot. Know it's a short-term investment, so spend deliberately.

Principle 3—NEVER CONFUSE COST WITH WORTH

Jesus says, "Do not store up for yourselves treasures on earth, where moth and rust destroy and where thieves break in and steal. But store up for yourselves treasure in heaven, where moth and rust do not destroy , and where thieves do not break in and steal. For where your treasure is, there your heart will be also" (Matt. 6:19-21).

What Jesus is saying is simple: Don't get too attached to your stuff. Don't love it. Don't need it. It doesn't last. It's an illusion.

Instead, value things that will last forever—God's Kingdom, His Word, people.

When I was a little girl, my Daddy always would say, "I only know of two things on this earth that will last forever—the Word of God and people." He said that over and over and over again until it was branded in my brain.

As of this writing my husband has been robbed 13 times. Our house has been broken into. Our car has been broken into. One time it was stolen altogether. Jeff was held up at gunpoint. Every single time the robbers wanted the same thing: stuff! They took his coat, my jewelry, a computer, a camera, a car radio, and on and on the list goes. One time, they actually stole a kitchen faucet—but it was always stuff.

Stuff never will last. It does NOT give us worth. It serves a purpose—but a finite purpose. Consider that when you buy something. What will this object cost me; is it worth it? That was really the essence of the argument that the couple had at the Spaghetti Warehouse; the husband didn't think that the stuff his wife was collecting was worth her taking a second job. Although the feminist inside me hates to side with the husband, in this instance, I have to admit he's right. He is worth more than that purse. Taking a second job meant taking away time from her husband. No purse or any other designer anything is worth that kind of sacrifice. It's not worth the cost.

Avoid the disastrous pitfall of falling in love with stuff. Instead, as flawed and thankless as they can be, fall in love with people. People last forever! They are precious in God's sight.

Principle 4—GIVE GENEROUSLY!

Generosity is the number-one characteristic that defines a godly spender. I first learned this quality from my childhood neighbor, Soraya. She lived across the street and in 1988 was a half-point away from making Brazil's Olympic gymnastic team. I always looked up to her. She instinctively was funny. She obviously was athletic. But the thing I remember most about Soraya is that although she was not the richest person I ever have known, she might be the most generous.

In the 1980s Brazil was in one of the worst financial crises in its history. It had incurred the world's largest foreign debt. Every citizen was paying the price in unemployment and high prices. Every day merchants would post new prices as things doubled in price on a weekly basis. One day my mother returned from the shoe store and commented she had just paid more for a pair of tennis shoes then she had for our refrigerator. In school we were learning how to do second-grade math word problems with millions because buying just a soft drink at the snack bar cost more than 1,000 Cruzeiros. The government actually changed the currency three times just to keep the zeros down. One time they just restamped the old money with a name and number. Everyone was broke. Although I didn't realize it at the time, my family, being American, probably was one of the richest families on our block.

But all over the world, kids are kids. We found scrounging up change for candy and soda pop to be our God-given duty. Most days, one or two of us would be successful in scrapping up coins for candy. The fortunate few would eat the cherished treats in front of the rest of us and maybe offered a bite or two to especially pitiful, wide-eyed friends. Nobody resented anyone for doing this. This was fair.

This, however, all changed after Soraya joined our little gang. Soraya was no richer than anyone else but had a childlike, instinctive penchant for egalitariasm. She would buy a bottle of cola (in those days, germs were of no concern) and would say, "OK, everyone gets one swallow." Then she would take a turn like the rest of us did, even though she had paid for the whole thing herself. One time, in front of me and another girl, she bought a hamburger and split the thing three ways—even though she was, by far, the biggest eater of the three of us and the purchaser of the prize. Once she took her frozen dessert bar and divided it up—one lick at a time—between four girls. No grownup was making her share. My mother would have had a conniption fit had she seen five children split a

98

single frozen treat. None of us even asked or expected Soraya to act this way. This was just the way she was. She just really never seemed attached to anything. She wanted others to experience whatever joy she was experiencing. She never had anything to prove.

Generosity usually is considered to be a virtue only the rich can afford. We expect those with great wealth to give out of the abundance of excess. Perhaps we believe they owe something to a world that has been so generous to them. However, in reality, the opposite tends to be true. The poorer someone is, the more likely that person is to be generous. Generosity is a state of character, not a condition depending on wealth.

Christians, by virtue of their place in Christ, would be thought to be the most generous people in the world. In the Old Testament, God tried to instill the act of giving into His people by commanding that they give a tenth of everything they had. This was God's way to support His work but also to teach faithfulness to His people. In the New Testament. Jesus never really talks that much about this tradition or about the concept we now call "tithing." He refers to it in a question about taxes, but it wasn't really a direct sermon. Is this possibly because "tithing" isn't important? Since Jesus was raised from the dead, we now live in a world that is saved only by the merciful grace of Jesus Christ and not by following a list of behavioral or religious rules. So, since we don't have to share our stuff to earn God's favor, does that mean we don't need to?

That, of course, could not be further from the truth. When a person gives his or her life to Jesus, that person gives all of it. That includes money. If Jesus is owner of all my stuff, then sharing it is no big deal. It's not mine to begin with. That means 10 percent is just the jumping-off point.

The day Jeff was mugged at gunpoint and was robbed of his coat, our friends from church joined together and collected money to purchase him another one. No one deducted this gift from his or her "tithe" to God. These people just gave out of the goodness in their hearts. When I had my first child, our church family threw me a shower and overwhelmed us with more baby paraphernalia than I knew even existed. I still use the rocking chair they gave us in those days when we had no money. Generosity is sharing what God has given you as God leads you to bless others. It's a lifestyle and a mentality, not some rigid rule a church may try to enforce to get the newest building project finished.

Giving generously is a blessing. People who give generously are noticed by the Lord and will not miss the money. I told the story of the financial scam in which Jeff and I were involved. Some months before we lost most of our savings, we felt led of God to donate $2,000 dollars to purchase a ticket for an African seminary student to go home and visit his family. At the time he had been away for a couple of years studying at the seminary across the street from my parents' home. Two-thousand dollars is a lot of money to missionaries fresh out of seminary, but we really believed this was God's will. We bought his ticket home. No more than a year later most of our funds had been obliterated. Had we had that $2,000, those funds would have been eliminated with the rest of our savings. Giving him that trip at the end of the year actually cost us nothing.

Jeff and I have learned to save systematically and build savings. It's important and good stewardship. Even though we do not make a lot of money by way of salary, God never has ceased to bless us. I could fill the pages of an encyclopedia writing out all the exciting and undeserved blessings I have received from the Lord—many by very extraordinary means. We have traveled the world, lived comfortably, and even taken our kids to Seaworld. I continually am shocked at the many blessings God never ceases to provide for me year after year.

In a spirit of recognition and thanksgiving for God's bounty toward us, we believe that being a blessing to others is our sacred obligation before an Almighty God. A man who is raising money to pay for his daughter's brain surgery approached my husband. Although fixing every person's financial needs is not our responsibility, Christ many times does ask us to get involved. In the case of this man, we did, but we could share many examples when we did not. It is a testimony of the Christ who lives in me. Being involved at home, in my community, and in the world is a testimony of the Christ Who lives in me. Being involved always costs time and cash.

God's will is not for Christians to give away everything they have. God's will is not for Christians to have nothing, because they donated to noble causes. Jesus reminds us, "The poor you will have with you always." Christ never laid on guilt.

God provides FOR us because He loves us. He deliberately blesses us with nice and wonderful things. HOWEVER, if we listen closely, He often desires to bless others THROUGH us. In fact a direct correlation exists. God chooses to bless us relative to His ability to bless THROUGH us. Simply no place in the kingdom of God exists for either a Scrooge or a hermit. Jesus says, "It is more blessed to give than to receive." As is often the case when Christ talks, He is speaking with a double meaning. Just think about it! From where do OUR blessings ultimately originate? They originate from Him.

Value 8

Choosing to Love

The night of the "Harvest Moon" had arrived. The entire dorm smelled of berry-fragranced mousse, hairspray, and perfume. Every door stood wide open as girls scurried around with towels on their heads and cotton balls between their nails. We were fixing each other's hair, putting on makeup, trading jewelry, and soliciting advice. It was our senior year and our last "Harvest Moon"—the name of the fall formal our social club sponsored each year.

This year was the first time I ever had attended the dance with an actual date. I had no date my fat freshman year. My sophomore year, I was a pledge and had to help organize the event. My junior year, I had been an exchange student in Kazakhstan. But this year, we all were here—our little group of girls who had pledged together and basically had lived together for the last four years. Everyone was excited. Everyone had interesting dates. It was our swan song!

Jeff called and asked if I could be ready 30 minutes early. I found that request odd but not really unusual. He probably wanted to swing through Taco Bell and fill up before heading to the formal. I was not really a primper and didn't take too long to get ready. Tonight, irony of irony, I was wearing a little black cocktail dress that I hadn't worn since my high-school graduation. It was short, it was sassy, and it felt timeless. I loved it.

Promptly at 6:30, the phone rang from the lobby. My date was ready to pick me up. In my stiletto heels I walked down the three flights of stairs, entered the lobby, and looked up to see Jeff's room-mate, Stuart, staring at me.

"Where's Jeff?" I asked. "What are you doing here?" I adored Jeff's roommate, but he was taking my girlfriend, Jeremi, tonight.

"I'm your driver. Get in the car." He was trying to hide the smirk on his face. My blood pressure started to soar. I sensed immediately what was happening. We drove to the top of the lookout over the Henderson campus—the other college in our small town. The lookout was the spot where Jeff first told me he loved me. When we got there, my roommate was sitting on the hood of her car. Smiling goofily, she still had rollers in her hair.

"Hey, Acorn (That's what they called me), I've got a note for you." Then she read me a little love poem Jeff had written. The poem gave me the directions to the next spot on my little treasure hunt.

Stuart drove me all over town as we went on a sort of "tour d'amour." We stopped at all the important places in Jeff's and my relationship. At every spot one of my sorority sisters was gleefully holding another note. Jeff had involved everyone I knew.

Finally we ended up at Jeff's tennis partner's apartment. Stuart drove off. My stomach was in my throat as I climbed the steps to where I saw the words "Chez Jeff" written on the door in Jeff's quirky handwriting. Inside I could hear the clumsy clanging of pots and pans. He was cooking. I smiled.

The door was slightly cracked. I saw Jeff standing in the kitchen with carrots and tomatoes in his hands. I had to laugh. He dropped the veggies and walked over to me. He was bearing 12 roses. "Hey, Sweetheart, we need to talk." He was smiling confidently. As I walked closer to him, he knelt down on one knee and said something beautiful and well-thought out. I actually don't remember very much of it. My head was spinning; everything was a blur. I remember the part at the end: "Christy Renee Akins, will you marry me?"

"Yes, yes, yes, yes!" I felt silly. Everything seemed so surreal.

We called my mother and told her what had happened. We called his parents. I helped finish making the dinner of salad, steak, and potatoes he was attempting to put together. We ate. I couldn't believe it—tonight of all nights.

"Jeff," I said toward the end of the meal after we had talked about the wedding date and other details, "why did you pick tonight? We are going to miss Harvest Moon." In retrospect that seemed like a horrible thing to say, but I was curious.

"We're not going to miss it. We're going to make an entrance."

That is exactly what we did.

We rode over to the DeGray Resort at which the dance was being held and arrived at just about the time everyone was finishing up dinner and taking pictures. My friends, who, of course, had told everyone at the dance what was going on, screamed like banshees when our car drove up. They ran out to take a glimpse of the ring. They grabbed our hands and rushed us to the front of the line to get our pictures made.

Everyone in the school congratulated us and wanted to see the ring. I felt like a star. Then I heard the disc jockey say, "And now I'd like to invite the future Mr. and Mrs. Jeff Brawner onto the dance floor for a congratulatory dance." I was floating on a cloud. I hardly knew how to dance. Now Jeff and I had the floor in front of the entire school. The DJ dimmed the lights and played some love song while the world watched us goofily pace around the dance floor. When the song finally ended, Jeff's fraternity brothers crowded around. They sat on the floor. I sat on Jeff's bent knee and listened to them sing the song I had heard them sing to every "Beta girl" who got dropped or engaged during the last four years. I knew the words by heart. "I wish I had a girl like you for dear BB. You are the sweetest girl in all the world to me. I love you. Adore you. I promise to be true. Beneath the sun, there's only one. And that one dear is you, just you . . .."

It was a night to remember. The next day, they put our picture in the college newspaper with the write-up about the dance. We even made the yearbook (something I had been unsuccessful at doing over the last four years). It was romance. It was true love— Sigh!

Or was it? Although I biasedly always will regard Jeff's proposal as the greatest proposal of all times, I have seen and known wonderful stories of romance that ended one year, two years, or six years down the road in bitter failure and misery. What is love? What does it look like? What does it feel like? The Bible, which has the answers to all of life's mysteries, seems somewhat limited in its list of love stories. We read about Isaac and Rebecca (not very romantic), Jacob and Rachel (which sadly ends in deceitful bigamy), and

Ruth and Boaz (a second marriage.) If love is one of the central themes of life, why does the Bible have no perfect fairy tale?

Then the answer occurred to me, Think BIG! The entire Bible is nothing but a love story!"

"For God so LOVED the world that He gave His only begotten Son, that whoever believes in Him should not perish but have everlasting life" (John 3:16).

For the longest time I thought that love was a feeling. It was the head rush when a cute boy looked at me from across the room. It was the thrill of being picked up in someone's car or given a rose. It was the kick in the stomach when getting kissed for the first time. When God created us for love, those were the things for which He created us—or so I thought.

A fundamental problem exists with this theory—it's not real! This understanding of love was something I had developed over years of watching Hollywood flicks such as *Notting Hill* or *Sabrina* (two of my personal favorites), or even reading the classic *Jane Eyre* (another favorite). It's just not real. It's a dream. It's an illusion. It is a cloud that looks pretty from far away, but if you try to sit on it, it makes the faithful tumble to the ground and land on something painful.

Love is not a feeling. It is a choice. It is a decision to honor someone. It is to value the life of someone else as more precious than your own. It is putting someone else before yourself. It is not something you will feel very often. It is not something you will "fall into." It is not something that is caused by broad shoulders and firm pecs. It is a selfless commitment that results in the deepest and most intense feelings in the world.

When I was in high school, I never really dated, but I did go out in groups with girls and boys—that is the Brazilian way. On one Halloween we had decided to go to a high-profile haunted house. We all crowded into a bus and headed downtown. When I sat down on my bench on the bus, I immediately realized that one new guy in the bunch had his eye on me. He sat by me. He chatted with me. He laughed at everything I said. I was flattered. We got off the bus and stopped for pizza before we went to the haunted-house show.

Although I don't remember for sure, I think the guy actually bought my pizza. I do recall that a street vendor who sold roses walked by the street cafe. The guy bought one for me. How romantic! He was working diligently to get some sort of kiss before the end of the night.

After we ate pizza, my "date" and I, along with the rest of the group, made our way over to the haunted house. My brother was teasing me. My friends all were acting goofy. This guy was laying it on thick. We stood in line and waited to get inside the house. Finally the sponsors divided us in groups of four and ushered us in. My "date" and I were in a group with two people we didn't know. Giggling, we started walking through the house, which was scary. I never had seen a house like this. It was pitch black. Live people were dressed up like dead people and monsters. The place smelled musty. Candles were lit everywhere. Realistic-looking skulls and bones were scattered around. We walked into the first room to see a "dead" person rise from a coffin. We stared for a moment and were making our way into the second room when a guy with fake blood gushing from his head and a hatchet in his hand came around behind us and screamed. When the monster screamed, I screamed. The other couple started running. Before I knew what happened, my "date" had rushed off into the darkness; I was alone. I turned looking for my "date" but instead felt the hatchet man put his hand on my shoulder. ARGHHHHHH! I ran straight through the haunted house and out the exit. I beat all the other groups out of the house. I never even saw my "date." Needless to say, that was the end of that romance!

Had we not gone to a haunted house that night, that guy may very well have talked me into believing he was "in love" with me. Who knows? He even may have believed it himself. He was attractive. He was attentive. He was a wonderful person, but he was not in love with me.

"For God so loved the world that he gave His only begotten Son." Love is selfless. Love is not about giving roses. It is not even about giving your time or body. Love is about giving of yourself. It is self-sacrificing. It is putting someone else in first place.

When Jeff and I first started dating, we were "in love". We nauseatingly wanted to spend every minute together. That is just what we did—to the detriment of all other relationships. But our relationship soon developed into something unhealthy. We always wanted something from each other. Before long these demands, although invited at first, transformed into burdens. In only a matter of time our relationship disintegrated into a charade of fights. We fought about everything. We fought so much and so often that I don't even remember what a single fight was about. In anger I once ripped Jeff's shirt off his back. I remember getting out of the car on the side of the highway and calling my roommate to pick me up. The most embarrassing fight occurred one night while we drove down a country road. When the argument got heated, Jeff had to pull off the road to concentrate more fully on the fight. When he did, he distractedly let the car fall straight into an embankment. Since this was in the days before cell phones, we had to put the fight on hold and stand out in the backwoods to wait for some truck to pass by and help us pull out Jeff's car. Finally, after what seemed like hours, a pickup did pass by. Two college students with ropes and chains in the back pulled us out of the embankment. They snickered to themselves and smiled at us. I'm sure they let their imaginations run wild as to how we had gotten that car in that embankment in the first place. It just made my blood boil. But here is the real irony. Jeff and I liked each other. We were attracted to each other. We wanted to spend the rest of our lives together, but we had not learned how to love each other. Our "love" was totally selfish.

Love means putting someone else first. "For God so loved the world that He gave His only begotten Son." How do we know that God loves us? We know that He loves us because He was sent to earth, He humbled himself, and He allowed himself to be crucified to pay the price for our sin. At a personal cost He paid a price we could not pay, so that we could live at peace with God and in freedom from sin. We know that He loves us because He looks out for our best interest. "I came to serve and not to be served," He said.

The Bible says that "God is Love" (1 John 4:8). Real love, the kind that springs from the heart of God, never is selfish. It never seeks its own. It suffers long. It does not envy. It does not behave rudely. It endures all things (1 Cor. 13:4-6). It involves trust.

How can a person find such true love? How do we know if we've found it? How do we give it?

Romantic love is a choice, so choose carefully. God chooses our birthfamily. Initially we instinctively love these members. Some families are close because, over the years, they have developed this love through time and commitment. Other families do nothing to nurture this basic relationship. Their love grows cold and stale.

However, romantic love is quite different. In most modern cultures we are involved in the selection process of the person with whom we ultimately will spend the rest of our lives. We are responsible. Most of us will spend fewer than 20 years living with our parents. You could spend upward of 60 years with your mate. Romantic love is more than a choice; it is one of the most important decisions a person ever will make. It will determine everything from where you live, to how you live, to whom you will be related, to what your children will look like.

For a decision so important, we are unwise when we base this choice on illogical reasons. We talk about it as though it's all about the "feelings"—the "electricity"—the "sparks flaring in the dark."

The truth is that nobody makes a decision about whom they will love based on "uncontrollable" feelings. We don't talk about it. We may not even realize it, but our attraction to a specific person reflects not our hormonal state or some sort of "chemistry"—but our values. If we see something in a person that is valuable, that person becomes attractive.

I learned this while I ate pizza in the Flippin-Perrin freshman dorm. Girls would return after their dates; we would sit around and evaluate the guys we had dated that evening. I still remember comments such as, "OOH, that guy is a catch. His father owns 'such and such' company." "He's related to the 'So and So's' of Northwest Arkansas." When we looked for dates, earning potential was of the utmost consideration. Bodies were discussed; personalities: sometimes; virtue or spirituality—never! Everyone wanted a "catch" that would make her look good. A girl's dorm-room evaluation reflected her values and priorities—usually her own future well-being and standing in a respectable community, hopefully close to home. The falling-in-love part would occur if the "catch" qualified. An outside observer easily could identify that the average resident of Flippen-Perrin valued a person that could provide a guaranteed income and place in society. This was what made some boys attractive and others not.

Falling in love involves emotions, but emotions always will follow the mind and our will. At some point emotions even may take over uncontrollably, but they are not the starting point. We pick people in which to invest time and emotions; we allow ourselves to "fall in love" with someone we admire for whatever reason, however noble or not. It could be looks, position, intellect, sense of humor, athleticism, spirituality, or any number of things. After we make a choice either consciously or subconsciously, we allow our emotions to get involved. This is the fun part, but it also is dangerous.

Emotions are by nature fickle. They play tricks on us and betray us. They NEVER can be trusted. The younger a person is, the more raw and more transparent are emotions. My youngest daughter is, by nature, a passionate person. Her emotions are strong. When she hugs me, I just tingle all over because she gives me the biggest kisses and says, "I wuv you a million and all the colors and all the numbers in the whole wide wold." However, in 30 minutes, after I have had to discipline her for something, she is capable of turning to me, looking me straight in the eye, and saying with all of her heart, "Yur the wost moder in the whole wide wold!" At that moment she absolutely means it with every emotion in her body. That is how she feels at that moment. She doesn't hate me, but she's young. Her emotions can overcome her. As a mother, part of my job is to help her discipline and control those very powerful feelings.

I have heard many women who have left their husbands say, "I just don't love him anymore." They say this as though they are the victims—as though things just can't be helped. They wish they still loved their husbands, but they can't. They would love him, but fate has robbed them of this love. This is all a lie and an excuse. Possibly and probably the electricity they first felt is gone.

However, true love is not electricity. It stands the test of time because it is not an emotion; it is a choice. It is a decision to love a person—no matter what the emotion of the moment may be (and emotions will run the gamut the longer you are with someone). We will love whomever we choose to love. That is the only way it can grow. I love my husband much more today than the day we got married. I love my children more today than the day they were born. I love my father more today than I did when I was a child. Love that is chosen grows steadily over time, because it is not based on emotions.

What "I don't love my husband anymore" means is "I love myself and think that I can do better on my own or with someone else." It means "I don't love you anymore because I choose not to." To me this is one of the most hurtful and most selfish things a person can say. It is betrayal in the most selfish sense of the word.

Romantic love involves selfless respect and absolute trustworthiness. Love that is healthy will grow over time. The "electricity" will ebb and flow, but the love itself will grow. When I met Jeff, I thought he was cute. I thought he was funny. I thought he was godly. I thought he was smart. He was the kind of guy with whom I wanted to spend the rest of my life. We started dating. We spent time together. We actually were foreign-exchange students together in Kazakhstan. However, as I look back, our "love" in the beginning was not selfless and really didn't involve trust. It was immature. The reason we fought all the time is that we each believed that the other person was trampling on our "rights." We weren't meeting each other's "expectations" of how we were to behave. After about a year of duking it out, we arrived at a truce. And our truce held up for about a year. After we got married, we were back to living in "love utopia."

Then, somehow our truce deteriorated back into all-out war. Jeff would leave a nasty spoon covered in peanut butter on the table all night long instead of washing it. My rights were violated because he knew that meant I was going to have to eventually pick it up and wash it. I would insist on flipping the lights off in our bedroom when I was sleepy, even though he wasn't tired and wanted to sit up to read. On and on went the litany of complaints from both sides. Some of it reads like ridiculous child play, but even the small stuff as we lived through it was real and "divorce-worthy."

The Bible has an answer for this. It wasn't one I really was ready to hear during my fits of rage. It says, "If your brother asks for your coat, give him your tunic, too." The biblical definition is, "To love means not just picking up the nasty peanut butter spoon but offering to wash ALL his dishes." "To love is always going to read in the other room every night." "To love means to deny your rights for the benefit of the other person, even if that person doesn't deserve it—even if it is not reciprocated."

This doesn't seem as though it would work. One particular day, I was cleaning the bathroom and looked in the floor to once again find Jeff's underwear lying right in front of the shower. I was irate. *If I don't complain, he'll never learn to pick up his clothes. I'll be picking up after him forever!* I thought to myself. I remember the silent voice of the Holy Spirit in my head saying, *Just pick them up and quit fuming.* Now I was just as angry at God. Didn't He understand that Jeff selfishly had left this underwear there? Jeff is the one with the attitude problem. But God was silent to my bickering. He seemed to say to me, "Your place is not to judge his selfishness. What about your own?" Jeff is God's child. God's job—not mine— is smoothing out his rough edges. My nagging not only was unproductive, it actually was sinful. God seemed to be saying, *If you spent as much time worrying about your own selfishness instead of His, you might not ever need to nag.*

I wish I could say I never nag him anymore. That would be a blatant lie. I wish I could say I'm not selfish. But I am trying. I did actually quit nagging about the underwear.

That is why, when you pick a mate, pick a person that you can leave to the Master's care—a person whom you can trust to God. More important, work diligently to be the kind of person that can be trusted completely. Each of us must decide in our own minds that even if my mate does not live up to his or her side of the bargain, I will be worthy of trust. Without this kind of unmerited commitment a loving relationship cannot develop. In any maturing relationship we many times feel as though the other person has acted selfishly without any consideration of our feelings. We will feel this way because it is probably the case. And when it is, we have an instinct to seek revenge—even for the small stuff. Over time, this leads to war. The truth is, we all have a history of living selfishly. In a true romance, both people work prayerfully toward a more mutual, selfless respect and absolute trustworthiness.

When I first started dating Jeff, he also was kind-of dating a girl back in his hometown. He did not hide this from me, as we were free to date other people. However, as time went on, I started to fall in love. I didn't want him to be dating some other girl. He actually never did go out with her, since she lived three hours away, but he hadn't bothered to cut off the relationship either. To make matters worse, she still was in high school. Months ago she had asked him to be her date to her senior prom. He was committed to going even though, by the time of the prom, our relationship was starting to get a little more serious. I really did feel as though he should honor his commitment to the girl. I trusted him to go to the dance. However, I didn't LIKE the arrangement at all.

The afternoon of the prom Jeff dropped me off at my dorm before he headed out to his hometown in his tuxedo. Before I got out of the car, I secretly (not telling him) dropped my earrings in the seat and left my lipstick in the glove compartment. This was all in a lame attempt to remind this girl that another girl had been in the car that day and that I was returning for my stuff! How silly! But this illustrates how selfish my "love" was. Jeff was MINE! It was all about ME. The Bible says in James 3:16 that "Where envy and self-seeking exist, confusion and every evil thing there are." Unfortunately Jeff and I have learned through some difficulty what loving someone selflessly means. We've run into lots of confusion and evil things. Having said that, over the last decade-plus of marriage and two-and-a-half years of dating, Jeff has done nothing but proven endlessly that he can be trusted. After all of this time together we love each other more now than we did during the early "fireworks" days. That's because our trust is greater. Our selfishness is less. I trust him to look out for my best interests. He trusts me to look out for his. Sometimes we mildly stab each other in the back as we stubbornly seek self-interest, but we are less likely now than we were in the beginning to be selfish. Our love has grown; it has deepened as the respect and trustworthiness have grown. And yes, I can still get goosebumps on dates!

God plans for every one of us to experience true love. The more we obey Christ, the more perfectly we can experience true love.

1 John 2:5 says, "Whoever keeps His word, truly the love of God is perfected in him."

No one is happy unless he or she is involved in relationships in which he or she feels loved. Love is the most basic need of humankind. We start experiencing it the minute we are brought into God's world. We need love because we need God; God is love. He built us to crave relationship with Him. The truth is that most of us search for romance and think it will satisfy this most basic need for love that we feel in the bottom of our guts. HOWEVER, no man, no matter how cute, rich, or smart as he may be, is God. No girl, however breathtakingly beautiful, truly can satisfy man's most basic need. No human ultimately can satisfy the need for love that is deeper than romance. Some women have kids to try to fill the void of love. But no baby, however sweet and dependent, can satisfy this need for love. Children also will leave us wanting.

Love flows downward in this sense. As we nurture a more intimate relationship with God through time spent daily with Him, He puts love—His love—in our hearts. His love does not depend on sex appeal, on the approval of peers, or even on our parents. It is God's love. Over time we become more capable of loving. We become more loveable. We become more selfless. God desires that each of us not only has a love relationship with Him but also loving relationships with other people. "Beloved, if God so loved us, we also ought to love one another" (1 John 4:11). God's plan is to fill this world with real love.

If we live in obedience to Him and allow God to guide and direct our lives, He will put people into our lives that we are meant to love. He will give us people that we enjoy loving—not hardship or charity cases.

I belong to that growing group of people that do not have what is traditionally called a "hometown." Since I turned 9, I have moved around. Most of the time I have lived in countries that were foreign to me. If I think about my shallow roots, feeling disassociated with the world and perhaps even lost would make sense. But this never has been the case. God always has put close friends and good people into my life at every juncture, from Washington D.C. to Shizuoka, Japan. This began in grammar school and progressed through graduate school, the work force, and the mission field. He put Jeff into my life; we were engaged two months before my mother passed away. He put two wonderful girls in my life that I'm privileged to have call me mother. He gave me amazing in-laws to whom I am close and a stepmother that I consider a close friend. I have moved around and been homeless for more than 20 years, but NEVER, NEVER, NEVER have I felt unloved.

The reason for this is not that I am so loveable; I'm not. It's not that I'm so lucky; I'm not. It's not even that I'm so spiritual; I'm certainly not. It's because I am loved first and foremost by my Father—the Lord Jesus Christ. I choose to love and follow Him because He first loved me. I trust Him because He is completely and totally trustworthy. Over time He teaches me to put Him first. As I grow closer to Him, I am becoming more and more selfless. Although I have a long way to go, He loves me in spite of my selfishness and takes care of my every need, both physical and emotional. Because He loves me and wants me to live in healthy relationships, He puts people in my life that love me—people who are trustworthy and people who are true. He allows me to "abide in His love" and feel it through the arms of others, no matter where I am. If we will value what He values; if we seek to love others in the way that He loves us, God will make sure love finds us.

Value 9

Choosing Romance

When I was in the ninth grade, my cousin invited me to go with his church on a canoeing trip. I didn't know anybody at his church, nor had I really ever been canoeing, but I decided to go anyway. When I arrived at the church, the youth minister asked everybody to pack into the two church vans parked in front of the gym. All the "cool" people, of whom my cousin was one of the coolest, piled into van number one. I, of course, was not cool and so was relegated to sit in van two. We loaded up and were about to head out when something unfortunate occurred in van 1. Right before we left, a "cool" girl showed up late and insisted on sitting in van one. A long conversation ensued between her and the youth minister. Finally one of the "cool" guys graciously gave up his place and rode with us on van two for the two-and-half-hours to the river.

The first few minutes of the ride were dull. Then people started to loosen up and talk. Somebody brought cards, so we played. Somebody knew riddles, so we struggled through those. In the two-and-a-half hours, we joked, laughed, and really just cut loose. The cool guy turned out to be really fun; he also was cute. He sat by me. We sort of flirted a little all the way there. I was having an absolute blast—much better than I had thought it was going to be while I loaded up in the "nerd van." I began to believe this trip was going to be awesome!

We finally got to the campsite and met up with the cool people from van one. "Cute Cool Guy" went back to be with his friends. I, who had no friends at all, just kind-of hung out to see to which tent the leaders would assign me. Some girls I had met in the van invited me to stay with them, so I unloaded in their tent and followed the group around the campground while we waited for supper.

During supper "Cute Cool Guy" from the van walked over and talked to me. We joked a little; then he dropped a bomb that changed the entire nature of this trip for me. Very nonchalantly he said, "Hey, tomorrow, we're going to be riding in two-person canoes." I said, "Yeah, I know." Then he said, "Would you like to ride in my canoe with me?"

When he said those words, a lead plate seemed to fall from the sky and just hit me across the head. I felt dizzy and immediately was speechless. "Well, yeah, uh, uh, sure. That sounds great." From that point on I was a nervous wreck. I lost my appetite. I lost my ability to speak. I lost my sense of humor. I turned into a complete blob—a very boring blob, at that. The next day "Cute Cool Guy" and I floated down the river, but that is about all we did—float. All day long I just couldn't think of anything to say to him. I felt awkward—just him and me and a bunch of water. Whatever question he asked me, my answer always was short and dull. I wasn't even the same person I had been the day before. This boy had done nothing but show kindness to me. But somehow, I felt as though I were on a "date." By "on a date" I mean "on trial." All of a sudden I felt as though this guy might not think I was pretty enough, cool enough, interesting enough, or skinny enough. Suddenly all I could think about was myself. I knew I was blowing whatever opportunity had been bestowed on me. I was destined to be tongue-tied!

The entire trip "Cute Cool Guy" was gracious. But that was the last time we ever spoke. In fact, he rode back to town in van one. He was a good friend of my cousin and turned out to be a great guy. However, I had successfully killed whatever "dating" experience I could have had—not because I was too short or ugly (which always were my primary fears). It was because I was a horribly awkward, self-conscious bore! I walked away from that canoe trip learning something very important about myself. I was horrible at dating!

Starting at about age 12, relationships with the opposite gender are very important. Small things such as going to movies can be remarkably stressful experiences. For most of us functioning in a two-gendered society is not easy. We feel the pressure of society's unreasonable expectations. They don't feel very natural.

For all of my growing-up years I always had tons of friends. I loved people: both boys and girls, but dating was different. On dates things never felt real to me. I couldn't seem to be myself. Endlessly I would stress over wanting someone to take an interest in me. But the moment I felt a spark of electricity, I felt as though the White Witch of Narnia had turned me to stone. I was overwhelmed with awkwardness. When an actual "date" was involved, I felt lost in a matrix!

Principle 1—DON'T MAKE IT ABOUT YOURSELF

This was my error on the canoe trip. Suddenly everything was about "me"! What was he going to think of "me"? Selfishness or self-involvement always breeds misery, fakeness, self-conscious-ness, and even hypocrisy. All this makes for a terrible date.

The Bible does not use the word *date*. In fact we would have to ask archaeologists and historians to describe the "dating game" as it existed in those days. However, many life principles in the Bible teach us how to relate to others. These principles apply to dating.

All throughout his various letters in the New Testament the apostle Paul discusses Christian behavior. His purpose is to teach us how to relate sincerely with each other. For example in Romans 12:9-10, Paul instructs that Christians should "Let love be without hypocrisy. Abhor what is evil; cling to what is good. Be kindly affectionate to one another with brotherly love, in honor giving preference to one another." It is straightforward advice for a good date. If I had applied this simple Bible verse to my canoe trip, I might have had a better experience.

"Let love be without hypocrisy." The word *love* here isn't refer-ring to romantic love. Instead it means that a person who is over-flowing with the love of Christ is a person that is AUTHENTIC. Authenticity is the opposite of hypocrisy. This means not pretending to be something or someone you are not. It means not worrying about being the "most" anything—be it the "most beautiful", "most engaging", "most intelligent", or "most impressive." It means being honest enough with God to allow yourself to be honest with others. It means thinking of the other person WITHOUT thinking about yourself. Instead of wondering about myself on the canoe trip and what kind of impression I was making, I could and should have focused my attention on the boy in the canoe. What was he like? What things interested him? What about HIM? Authenticity brings freedom. Transparency brings freedom. Above all God has called us to a life of freedom!

"Abhor evil, cling to what is good." Because dating tends to be so much about making impressions and about being "cool", often one is tempted to lower one's moral standards, since evil is cooler than goodness. Pursuing goodness on a date may be a challenge, but clean fun makes for better memories. On a date, plan interesting activities that are pure and innocent—those things that could be described as "good."

"Be kindly affectionate to one another with brotherly love." Everyone has heard of the term "trophy wife"—the "Anna Nicole Smith" an old man buys to showcase to all of his equally old and ugly friends! However, I've never heard a term for what girls notoriously and most commonly practice throughout their entire lives—the "she-who-has-the-best-date-wins!" game. "Best date" means "he who makes me look the best in front of my friends." We look for boys who will spend gobs of money on us, take us to expensive restaurants, drive us around in fancy cars, or treat us in a way that will impress our friends.

Besides creating an incredibly competitive environment, playing the "best-date" game at school or at work is extremely selfish, ungodly, cruel, and unfair to boys. "Be kindly affectionate to one another with brotherly love" means be nice and treat someone as if he were your younger brother—tenderly, affectionately, thoughtfully. It means offering to pay for stuff. It means thinking of the other person as a person and not as a "date" or as a key to "social status." It means not looking at a relationship with the attitude of "what is in it for me?" It means kindness.

"In honor giving preference to one another"—Honor: everyone wants to feel honored. I want to believe that the person I am with really respects me for my strength, intelligence, courage, or any other honorable attribute. We want to walk away thinking, "I really impressed this person." People who are good dates are those who attempt to build up their dates—playing to strengths. Those who are good dates notice the kind things done to impress and appreciate the details. They appreciate the money being spent or the thought that went into the preparation. Those who are good dates smile and are proud of the person escorting them. A good date is not self-involved in thinking about how this date will play back with the gang but will spend this mental energy trying to make the other person feel good about who he/she is as a person. A good date does this regardless of whether the relationship has a future.

Preference—thinking of the other person. In my dating history I took a long time in learning how to simply focus on the other person. About what does the person like to talk? What are the person's interests? What is fun for the individual to do? Make it not about you! When you live unselfishly, you allow yourself not to live self-consciously. ME is not as important as YOU. When dating can become about YOU and not about ME, it can start being fun.

Principle 2—DON'T MAKE IT ABOUT SEX

"As a ring of gold in a swine's snout,
So is a lovely woman who lacks discretion" (Prov. 11:22).

A pig with a nose ring! What an interesting mental image! Pigs stink. They are ugly. For a Jew they serve absolutely no practical purpose, since Jews don't even eat pork. What could be more useless than to put an expensive piece of jewelry in the snout of a pig?

Most English-translation Bibles use the word "fornication"—a big, Shakespearean word that simply means "voluntary sexual intercourse between two unmarried persons." From the time he turns 13 sex is on every boy's mind. It's simple biology. This doesn't make a boy "evil" or "sinful." That's how God designed boys. Boys have a sex drive that is on auto-pilot! They notice the figure of every female in a room, no matter the person's age or size. A computer couldn't be more effective. As boys grow and mature, they learn how to control and direct all the energy and aggression that springs from this. As they mature in Christ, the Lord teaches them self-discipline in all areas of life as they learn to discipline their sex drives.

Girls, however, are wired differently. Sex is about emotions. It also is about power. Seduction can be fun, because a rush occurs when the emotions rise up the charts. Girls can feel powerful as they realize they can manipulate boys through the male sex drive.

However, from the beginning of the Bible to the end, God condemns sex outside the context of marriage. "Flee sexual immorality. Every sin that a man does is outside the body, but he who commits sexual immorality sins against his own body. Or do you not know that your body is the temple of the Holy Spirit who is in you, whom you have from God, and you are not your own? For you were bought with a price therefore, glorify God in your body and in your spirit, which are God's."

This seems so old-fashioned. It seems so stuffy—sex only in marriage. The older one gets, this especially seems ridiculous. One might think, *I'm almost 30 years old; God can't possibly want me to remain celibate forever!* However, it really is a straightforward issue. God says to save sex for the marriage bed.

Jeff and I met when we were 17 years old. We started dating when we were 18. Jeff grew up in Wynne, AR. I was a Yankee who had spent half of her life in South America. Our backgrounds were totally different; with one exception—both of us had committed our lives to the Lord. I was little when I decided to follow Christ. Jeff was 17 when he accepted the Lord. This decision changed things for both of us. When I accepted Christ when I was a child, sex definitely was not on my brain, but as I grew up, I began to understand that living in obedience to Christ involved sexual purity. Jeff was older, but he also made a similar commitment and stayed true to it despite the pressure.

God has lots of reasons why He desires for His children to remain sexually pure: disease, success at marriage, kids born parentless, intense emotional bonding, on and on the list goes. When God says, "your body is the temple of the Holy Spirit . . .You are not your own . . . Glorify God in your body and in your spirit, which are God's", He doesn't open any parentheses for exceptions (long engagements, divorcees that already are sexually active, marriages wreaked by havoc, teen-agers who have been together since they were 13). I feel God is trying to say, "My child, if you can trust Me with your eternal destiny, can you not trust Me with your body? I love you. I know you better than you know yourself. I know what you need. I know your dreams. Give them to Me; allow Me to glorify Myself through you."

Abstinence can feel wrong in a society that equates love with sex and number of sexual partners with sexiness. If we allow God to control our sex lives and abstain from sex until marriage, will we waste the greatest years of our life—our youth? Won't we lose out on fun, romance, and excitement during the years when all this is most attainable? The truth is the opposite: sex outside of marriage ultimately ruins romance!

I have a childhood friend that totally disagrees with me about premarital sex. She finds my beliefs old-fashioned and churchy. "Sex can be controlled. My emotions can be controlled. Sex is just about having fun," she maintains. She believes this and lives this out. One night, in particular, I remember she was invited to go out on a date. She was meeting a particular guy for the first time and was excited about the prospects. She got in the car with the boy, who told her they were going to the mall and to a movie. After a few minutes in the car, somehow through the course of the conversation, he figured out that she wasn't a virgin and drove straight past the mall to a motel, where they spent the rest of the evening. She told me she had fun. I suspect she did. However, she did not experience romance. She certainly didn't experience love. The boy didn't last through the month.

Sex and romance are not the same thing. Love and sex are not the same thing. In fact, if sex is not dealt with in the way God designs, it destroys both romance and love.

Girls do not go out with boys to get sex. This may be Hollywood window-dressing, but it is not real. Girls desire relationships. They desire passion. They desire emotion-filled romance. Most desire to experience love. Ultimately both boys and girls want this, even if sex sometimes is too much on the male brain for boys to think clearly while they shake under a strobe light on a dance floor.

"A ring of gold in a swine's snout"—Why would Solomon say that about a loose girl? He says this because being sexually promiscuous is not attractive. It may be sensual and lusty. It actually may get a girl lot of dates, but it is not attractive in the sense that it does not create love.

Nobody falls in love with a pig. Even if you put a gold ring in its nose, it still is a stinky pig. That's what Solomon is saying about promiscuity. A person is not just flesh. You are composed of a spirit and a soul as well. If someone is going to fall in love with YOU, he will fall in love with all of you: your body, your mind, your soul. If all he loves is the flesh, it's like loving the nose ring of a pig while you despise the pig.

Physical attraction feels dangerous; that makes it fun. It is part of the game God invented to bring boys and girls together. However, to play the dating game successfully, avoid the pitfall the Bible calls "fornication." Don't allow sex to enter the dating relationship. Although doing so may feel stupid, talk about sex before the relationship grows into an emotional bond. Having a fundamental understanding of where each person stands on this issue is important, or else, things will be awkward. The boy will start thinking sex from the very first passionate kiss, even if he's committed to sexual purity. As soon as the hormones kick in, he will immediately and instinctually start thinking about naked flesh. All else is a blur. The only reason a boy restrains from having sex every time he kisses a girl is love. That seems ironic, because in the height of passion, all kinds of hot air may proceed from his mouth—hot air such as, "OH, I love you. I want you. I treasure you! You're the most beautiful woman in the world." But that's all testosterone. The true expression of love is the opposite: he will refrain from sexual promiscuity because he loves God and wants to honor God with his body. A boy isn't the wrong boy because he wants sex. He was designed to want it. He's the wrong boy if he wants it and doesn't honor the God and the girl enough to wait for it. True love is selfless. True love is not easy. A boy who can be trusted for life is a boy that can show sexual restraint. A girl who can be trusted is a girl who will not use sex to manipulate a boy.

The problem for most is that when love is involved, we live in a dream world—a place we've built for ourselves out of scenes from our favorite chick-flicks, pages from our favorite romance novels, and lyrics from romantic rock songs. But, in a dating relationship, although the emotions are fun, they must be checked by respectful actions. A real relationship cannot be built on empty words. The Song of Solomon probably is one of the most famous love poems ever written. It is about beauty. It is about sex. It is a picture of true love as God Himself envisions. Sadly for Solomon, in his personal life, these merely were words. Solomon had more than 1,000 sexual partners. He was king for 40 years. That means, if Solomon took a new wife and/or concubine on a regular basis during the course of his reign, he had a new girlfriend every two weeks. The Shulamite, the object of Solomon's desire in the Song of Solomon, is not even mentioned in any of the historical books of the Bible. God showed Solomon what true love really could be. It was his for the taking, but Solomon never allowed God to realize that reality in his life. For Solomon, it was a lost opportunity. If the goal of dating is to find true love, create an environment in which true love will sprout. If we don't, we have nothing but what Solomon had: a beautiful vision and a failed dream.

Principle 3—"DON'T AWAKEN LOVE UNTIL IT PLEASES"

"I charge you, O daughters of Jerusalem,
By the gazelles or by the does of the field,
Do not stir up nor awaken love
Until it pleases" (Song of Solomon 3:5).

One day when Elizabeth was 4 years old, I went to school to pick her up and watched her play with her buddies on the playground.

123

As I stood there, one of her teachers approached me. "Do you know Victor in Lizzy's class?" the teacher asked me.

"Yes, the little blond boy over there by the slide. Why?" I replied.

"Well, Victor has told the entire class that he is Lizzy's boyfriend. He tries to sit next to her at lunch and at the craft table. He makes her very uncomfortable. I don't think she likes it, but we all find it funny."

In my mind this after-school playground conversation explained a very confusing dialogue I had had with Elizabeth a few days beforehand. Totally distressed and worried, she had approached me. "Mommy," she said, "I think I'm going to have to marry a girl."

"Why do you think that, Lizzy?" I asked her.

"Well, it's just that except for Daddy, I don't like boys."

I had a tough time keeping a straight face, but I picked up my distressed baby girl and said, "Well, don't worry about that right now. You're not old enough to get married. You just might change your mind later. But, if it makes you feel better, you don't have to get married at all. You can just live with me forever, OK? Now, want to play Candyland?"

It's humorous. Of course Elizabeth was too young to worry about boys. She was 4 years old. But could this possibly be how God looks at us when he sees us worrying about whether we will die a virgin or never find true love? When God breathes life into us, He creates us for eternity. We have a beginning, but we have no end. From God's eternal perspective, 30 years old is not that different from 4 years old. Just as the fastest ant in an ant race is not all that much faster than the slowest, the difference is irrelevant in His view of the overall picture.

Some of us will get lots of dates over the course of our lives. My running buddy in high school, Becky, always got three times more dates than I did. In college, my roommate, Amy, always showed me up as well. She was every boy's dream date: tall, leggy, blonde, curvaceous, and fun. I never was as lucky as Becky or Amy. I would get dates from time to time, but that wasn't to be the center of my social life. If I had counted on snaring a date in order to go to homecoming, I might or might not even attend the event—much less attend it with someone I actually wanted to be with. But as I commiserate over my own mediocre social agenda, I know some girls never have been on a date—EVER.

This is the biblical advice: don't allow your self-image to get confused with the number of dates you get. Live the life you were given to live. Enjoy every minute of it. God created you for joy, for freedom, and for love. He has a plan that will play out perfectly if you obey Him. Not all of us will be big daters. That's just fine. Don't spend your youth worrying about the next date.

Don't allow your self-image to be related solely to the person hanging on your arm. When you go on a date, go for the fun of it. Don't believe that the only fun in the world is found in games with the opposite sex. It's not. Going out usually is more fun in groups or pairs, so go with friends. It will relieve some of the sexual tension. Don't force yourself to fall in love just because you think you should, that the time to do so has arrived, or it's the fun thing to do.

My mother always was a Christmas fanatic. She loved Christmas and made it the main event of every year. She spent months making decorations, collecting exotic ingredients for delicious foods, and—of course—started her Christmas shopping early. Every year she would hide our gifts in the same place. Most years, she was finished with all of her shopping before December even rolled around. My brothers and I joked that we knew exactly where she would hide everything—from the candy for our stockings to the gifts for under the tree.

One year, I thought I would be sneaky. I waited for an afternoon when my mom was out of the house. Then I went to her secret hiding place, dug out every gift, and proceeded to open them. Some of them were great. Others I really didn't even like. I left no gift unopened. But of course, before my mother returned from her outing, I repackaged everything just as I had found it. To this day I don't know if my mother ever knew that I opened those gifts that year. I thought I was so funny and clever. All day long I knowingly laughed to myself.

However, Christmas eventually rolled around. My little brother was jumping on me to get out of bed and open gifts. The house, full of overnight guests, was a frenzy. Everyone was excited and looking forward to seeing what was hidden under the tree. To this day I remember rolling out of bed and smiling. I even remember giggling, but that year, for the first time ever, I remember feeling nothing. I felt no excitement. I knew no surprises awaited. I knew everything that was going to happen. I had opened everything in secret. I didn't feel guilty. Truthfully, I was mad at myself. I had cheated myself out of one of the fulfilling experiences of the Christmas season— opening gifts as a family. Others were sharing excitement. I was being fake. I never have forgotten that Christmas, because I learned an important lesson: never open your presents early, even if you know where they are. Doing this is just not worth it.

"Don't awaken love until it pleases." It means, don't open your Christmas presents before Christmas. Guard your heart. Don't give it away to the first person that walks through your door. Allow love to arrive and play its game with your heart in its own time. Go out, socialize, have fun, but guard your emotions and guard your body. Fall in love with the right person on God's terms. Be patient; know that one day the wait really will be worth it.

Value 10

Conquering Fear

When I was a little girl, we lived in a white, two-story, wood-framed house on busy Allentown Road in Oxen Hill, MD. Two blocks up from our house was the fire station. A little further up the road was the police station.

My bedroom was completely wallpapered with pink flowers. Across from my bed was a huge window overlooking our front porch. Next to my bed was a walk-in closet. My mother kept all my beautiful Sunday dresses, my roller skates, and my stuffed animals and dolls inside it. My room was right by the front door, which was directly in front of the stairs. Mine was the only bedroom on the first floor; my parents and brothers both had bedrooms upstairs. In typical '70s fashion, our entire house, including my room and the stairs, were covered with "grass-stain" green shag carpet. I loved this house with its vegetable garden and swing set in the back yard. I loved its largeness, my pink bedroom, the big tree I could climb all by myself, and the porch swing in front of my window.

However, every night as the sun went down and darkness crept into my room through my front window, this beautiful utopia suddenly turned haunted. Cars routinely passed by. When they did, their headlights would shine through the shade on my window. They sent ghosts soaring across my room and me headfirst under my sheet. The fire trucks screamed when they sped down the street. Soon after them the police cars and the ambulances shrieked. Each unique shrill could shoot chills down my back. But the worse part about the night was the alligator-monsters that hid behind my dolls inside my closet.

Soon after my mom or dad would kiss me good-night, these monsters would poke their bulging eyes and snarling teeth out from under the dolls in my closet. The green shag carpet would magically transform itself into water. The monster-alligators would swim

127

across my room and slither around my bed. They would lurch all night and only left me alone when the early rays of sun would peek through my curtains. In my heart I knew that if I ever put one foot on the floor, one of the monster alligators would bite off my leg or worse—eat me. My imagination soared. I almost could feel the alligators swirl around and snap their teeth in the darkness. I could feel the ghosts fly across the room.

In the morning, however, I would wake up. It all would be gone. I would stare blankly at the innocuous shag carpet and empty walls. No monster alligators? I knew ghosts weren't real. I was almost the same age as Pippi Longstocking. She wouldn't have been afraid! How could I be so silly? But the very same night I inevitably would go through the same routine again. I would try to be brave but would fall to my illogical fears.

This went on until one fateful night I woke up needing to go to the bathroom. I looked around; sure enough, a ghost stared at me from the top, right-hand corner of my room. I pulled the covers up to my neck and listened for the alligators, who were eager to nibble at my toes and stuck their heads up out of the shag carpet. Gripped with fear I lay in bed: Should I make a mad dash for the bathroom up the stairs? To get there I would be forced to cross an entire ocean of alligators. If I didn't, I was sure to wet the bed. Wetting the bed felt too humiliating. I had to face the creatures and climb the stairs.

I still remember standing on top of my bed and staring down at the green shag carpet stocked with creatures. I formulated a plan. If I could jump from alligator to alligator and only step on their heads, they couldn't eat me. I might travel unharmed across the room and up the stairs to the safety of the tile-floored bathroom. I collected my nerve and, as quickly as I could, hopped from gator head to gator head across my bedroom, then up step by step to the bathroom tile. Exhausted, I gasped for breath after making the last plunge and landing on my knees. I felt a wave of relief. I had made the trip in one piece. After I flushed the toilet and washed my hands, I looked down the stairs at the long journey back to bed. Was I lucky enough to make the journey safely a second time? For a few seconds I thought and then decided I could do better. I walked across the hall into my parents' room and over to my mommy's side of the bed. I poked her on the shoulder, woke her up, and said, "Mommy, can I sleep with you?" She groggily looked at me, "What is it, Baby? What are you doing up?"

I thought about admitting to her my visions of ghosts and alligators but just said, "Mommy, I'm scared." My mother gave me a kiss and a hug and said, "Baby, you have nothing to be afraid of. Go back to your room and get in bed." Then she rolled over and drifted back to sleep.

I still remember staring at the back of her head. I had no choice but to face the monsters. I remember voicing a short prayer and asked God to make me not afraid, so down I walked. This time I did not race or jump. I just walked. In my imagination I could feel the alligators swimming around my feet, but I ignored the visions in my head and just kept walking down the stairs until I fell into my bed. My muscles didn't relax until I safely was tucked under my quilt and my eyes were closed. I didn't smile, but I did feel good about myself. I had won.

Everyone probably has a similar story of a childhood fear based on nothing more sinister than too many episodes of "Scooby-Doo." As we grow up, we discard these phobias as no more than memories of childish foolishness. However, if we think back to how we felt, we are forced to admit that the fears are gripping. They are consuming. Years later we still can recount with precision specific reoccurring nightmares, flashing lights, creepy stairs, creaky doors, musty basements, or just the smell of darkness. These are memories carved from our fears.

The alligators were not to be my last confrontation with the monster in my closet. As I grew up, fear metamorphosed into a social monster. When I was in the sixth grade, I began attending a mega-sized, Brazilian junior-high/ high school. I didn't speak Portuguese very well and knew no students in my school. I had to wear a uniform and, for the first time, carry books back and forth for seven different classes with different teachers. This, in itself, was enough to horrify an 11-year-old, but the story was more than that. My Portuguese teacher was a beautiful but stern, unsmiling woman with bright red hair. Her name was *Dona* Raquel. She carried a box of chalk and her roll book with her wherever she went. She made us sit in alphabetical order and never called us by our names—just by our numbers in her dreaded roll book. I was number 11.

Every day *Dona* Raquel would enter our classroom and in deathly silence begin writing our assignment on the board. Every day we would copy long texts from our literature book. Then she would call out numbers from her roll book to read aloud the copied text. I was mortified and dreaded the day she would call my number. I couldn't read well.

One day, not too long after the beginning of school, she told us the time had arrived to begin our grammar lessons. Within the next seven days we must purchase our text, entitled the *Novíssima Gramática*. She warned us that if we didn't bring our grammar books within the week, we would be called to stand alone in front of the class and receive an oral examination over the point of grammar reviewed that day.

I was horror-struck. My mother turned over the city looking for the *Novíssima Gramática*. By the specified day I still did not have my copy. I cried all night. In fact I deliberately tried to stay up and make myself physically sick before the dreaded deadline. I did NOT want to face that woman grammarless.

The next morning I pretended to be ill. My parents were sympathetic but unfooled. Like I did every other day, I must walk to school. I still remember my mother saying, "Face your fears, Christy. Never run!" Knowing that I must be empty-handed as I faced the red-haired fiend, I climbed the two flights to class. I most certainly would be the only person without a grammar book. Death by public humiliation was inevitable. As I went up each step, my body felt heavier and heavier. I turned and stared into the room. I saw her clutching her roll book and ready to check our grammars. I entered the room and walked to my seat. Whatever was going to happen, I was there to face it. In this case, it turned out to be a bluff. *Dona* Raquel had no intention of carrying out her threat.

Facing down my fear of that Portuguese teacher was a lesson that I never forgot. But even that did not cure me from this nagging evil called "fear." This evil just continued to change forms and got craftier and smarter as I grew older and braver.

The first year my husband and I were career missionaries, we lived in the state of São Paulo with our brand-new baby girl, Anna Katherine. We were excited about "changing the world." We felt fearless and invincible. One block away from our house sat what the Brazilians call a *favela*—an urban slum in which people build their own houses from things such as mismatched panels, bricks, or cardboard. *Favelas* are filthy places filled with crime, drugs, and darkness. Being that God placed us so close to this *favela*, we believed our mission must be to tackle it head-on. Twice a week Jeff went into this area with our neighbor he had led to Christ. They offered Bible studies to people our neighbor knew through his drug habit. Over the course of time a small group of believers started meeting together; a church was born. We were elated. God was at work there after all!

One day, however, one of the members of this little group stopped by and told us that he needed cash and really wanted to wash our car. We were heading out the door and foolishly told him we were leaving. We asked him if he could return the next day. He agreed. That night, while we ate dinner at a friend's house, that young man and some of his friends broke into our house. They jumped our wall, hack-sawed through the metal bars on our window, and busted into my bedroom. With their nasty feet they stepped all over my new bedspread.

We returned from dinner to find glass from the window pane smashed all over the bed and strewn across the room. The closet doors were opened. Jeff's office was trashed; everything we owned of value was gone. My jewelry, our camera, and our computer were gone. They had tried on our clothes and eaten our food. Jeff spent the rest of that night at the police station. He stood in lines and filled out reports. I spent the night staring at the hole in the bars inches from where I laid my head to sleep.

From that night on I began my worst battle with fear. My fear was not that robbers would enter my house and steal more of my stuff. My fear was that they would find me home and, when they did, would kill me and steal my baby. I had nightmares. I felt pain in my chest. I booby-trapped my house with dishes in the hall and chairs against the doors to wake me if anything were to happen. I moved our daughter's crib into our room.

Three months later we moved more than 2,000 miles to a new home in Fortaleza. Fear followed me. Our new home ironically was one block away from a *favela* in our new town. Fear overwhelmed me when, not long after our arrival, a thug jumped our wall and stole things out of our front yard. I was living a nightmare. I tried to thief-proof my new house. I put up electric wires around the perimeter of the nine-foot wall that surrounded our house. On our doors we installed traps that would set off an alarm if they were forced open. I installed motion sensors in the living and dining rooms. We even put in panic buttons connected with security-service personnel that would run to our place with guns if anything were to happen. But all of these precautions didn't take care of the fear.

Fear had dug his fangs deep within me and built a home in my heart. No external contraption had any power to relieve me from his strangling presence. I was losing a battle—not with the bad guys outside my gate but with the monster inside my heart. Finally I realized fear was in my spirit. This fight was spiritual warfare! I understood what Franklin Roosevelt meant when he said, "We have nothing to fear but fear itself." The problem was that fear was stronger than I.

When we are afraid—be it at age 7 with imaginary alligators, in junior high in front of a crowd, or in fear for our children's lives— we are in torment. 1 John 4:18 says, "Fear involves torment." Fear taunts us. It tortures us. It paralyzes us. It humiliates us. It breaks our will and forces even strong people to their knees in tears of anguish. Fear is real. It's not just a figment of our imaginations! Fear attacks everyone: the young and the old, the strong and the weak. As a teen-ager King David actually killed a lion while he watched sheep, but in the psalms we see him gripped with fear. The combatant apostle Paul fearlessly faced down governors, soldiers, and even poisonous snakes, but in Acts 18:9, God tells him to not be afraid. Each person can learn how to win the battle and defeat this monster within.

The first step is to realize that fear does not originate from God. The apostle Paul tells Timothy in 2 Timothy 1:7, "For God has not given us a spirit of fear, but of power and of love and of a sound mind." The opposite of fear is power, love, and a sound mind. When we are afraid, we feel absolutely powerless. We feel alone; we feel as though we've lost our mind. When I was stacking chairs against the door that led into our hallway, I knew I was acting on the brink of insanity. When I heard noises on my street and imagined criminals climbing the walls into our yard, I might as well have thought they were my childhood "ghosts" flying across my room. God does not want his children to live in fear. 1 John 4:18 says fear involves torment. Torment emanates from the pit of hell. But how do we overcome it? Can we just face it down? Do we just "buck up?" What is the secret to facing the truly evil monster with his fangs deep inside our hearts?

In 1 John 4:18 the Bible says, "There is no fear in love, but perfect love casts out fear." In 1 John 4 He says for us to abide in His love. If we abide in His love, His perfect love will cast out the fear in our hearts. The second step to living without fear is learning to abide in God's love. But, what does that mean? How do we abide in God's love?

Throughout his writings the apostle John goes into great detail to explain this, but in summary John 15:10 says, "If you keep my commandments, you will abide in my love." The short answer is simple: obey God. Stay away from evil, just as He instructs us to do. Spend time with Him by practicing the most basic discipline of the Christian faith: meditation on God's Word. To this very day I end every day reading Scripture. I started this as a child because as I began to read the Bible, I noticed that I rarely had nightmares on those particular nights. Of course a Bible is not a charm that will chase away all of the ghosts in our closets, but when we mediate on God's Word, it seeps inside our spirits. Fear has more difficulty finding its way inside us. We are insulated. We have a defense. But reading the Bible is only one part of keeping God's commandments. Learning to obey God involves a lifetime of discipline. During the entire year after our robbery I was paralyzed with fear. I continued to pray and read my Bible every day. I was involved in social projects in our community. I was a Baptist missionary living in a foreign country. But all of these things, as noble as they were, were not enough. Ephesians 6:12 tells us that when we do battle with "powers, against the rulers of darkness, against spiritual hosts of wickedness", we need more than the Sword of the Spirit. We need the whole armor of God.

Some people have interpreted the phrase "keep my commandments" as a command to live a perfect life, or at least to appear to live a perfect life. Not only is that impossible, it is hypocritical. If we actually try to live that kind of life, we have to be dishonest with ourselves. Keeping God's commandments only can be done by waking every morning and dressing ourselves in the "whole" armor of God.

What is the whole armor of God? It is truth, the breastplate of righteousness, preparation of the gospel of peace, above all the shield of faith, and the Sword of the Spirit, which is the Bible. To live a life of power, love, and a sound mind, the final step is to make a lifetime commitment to perfecting ourselves in the science of using spiritual weaponry. Embrace all these things.

Truth: live a life that is transparent—no secrets. Don't pretend. Even if it will embarrass you or make someone mad, if you have made a mistake, own up to it. Bring it out into the light of truth. Truth has freedom in it. I can't live in the darkness of secrecy. Darkness is scary. Bad things always happen in the dark. Don't revel in darkness. Live in truth—in the light in which truth dwells.

Breastplate of Righteousness: live a life that is correct. Basically, righteousness means doing what is right. Making right decisions requires practice, not to mention nerves of steel, but it is freeing. God gives us the strength to do it. When we are doing right, we eliminate a host of fears. Truth has power in it. Doing what is right requires courage. Things don't affect us nearly as much when we know we did the right thing. Over time, as we practice righteousness, we can nurture an ability to be bold.

Preparation of the Gospel of Peace and **Helmet of Salvation**: When a person ask Jesus into his or her heart, then that person knows for sure that God is on his or her side—no matter what. That is why the gospel is unique: it can provide true peace in our souls. Giving their hearts to the Lord Jesus Christ gives persons peace and eternal security. I can have confidence that my life is His and that ultimately He's in control. I feel as though I have a helmet over my head. Giving control over all of life's situations to Christ is peaceful because He is prepared. He is capable of preparing me and sustaining me. Giving one's heart to the Lord is the first step in any venture that will involve God. He accepts nothing short of total commitment.

The Shield of Faith: Faith is not magic. It is NOT saying something and God's doing whatever I said, assuming I believed strongly enough. In the fairytale *Peter Pan*, a fairy dies every time someone says that fairies aren't real. At one point in the story Tinkerbell dies. The only way for her to become resurrected is for children all over the world to believe in fairies. At this point in the story the reader stops and chants with the child with whom he or she is reading the story, "I do believe in fairies! I do believe in fairies! I DO BELIEVE IN FAIRIES!" This recitation has the power to resurrect Tinkerbell. This, of course, is what happens. Tinkerbell lives on to save Peter Pan and Wendy from the sinister Captain Hook.

This is NOT an example of faith. Faith is not creating magic by virtue of belief. Faith is a synonym of TRUST. To have faith is to trust in God enough to do what He says to do. The bottom line for fear is the unknown future. *What will happen to me if . . .?*

The scary truth always will be that no one has any certainty of the future. It is always outside of our grasp, no matter what palm-readers or psychics claim to know. Not even Satan nor any angel in the spiritual realm is privy to this information. Only God in His sovereignty knows the future. No human ever will know his or her own fate. Ultimately this fact is the source of our fears. That is why submission to God is better than rebellion. Our future is in Christ's hands. That is why David could say in Psalm 23, "Yea, though I walk through the valley of the shadow of death, I will fear no evil, for You are with me." He trusted God. David knew his future was entirely in God's hands. He knew that even if he walked so close to death that he actually could feel death's shadow, he still would be unafraid because God was with him. In Psalm 27 he says, "The Lord is my light and my salvation; Whom shall I fear? The Lord is the strength of my life; Of whom shall I be afraid?" In Psalm 118 he concludes that, "The Lord is on my side; I will not fear. What can man do to me?" Through the course of His life, he learned—mostly through running from bad guys and sleeping in caves—that he could trust God.

The God of David still is alive. We, too, can walk so close to death that we feel its shadow and still be unafraid when we learn to abide in His love and trust Him. We can believe that God really will take care of us when we walk in obedience to Him. A shield of protection exists in this kind of faith. Trust Him who is in control.

1 John 4:18 says, "There is no fear in love, but perfect love casts out fear, because fear involves torment." No person, of course, is the owner of perfect love. Only God is the creator of perfect love. But in 1 John the writer explains that God is in the process of perfecting His love in us. We see a direct correlation in the fact that the closer we walk to the Lord, the more His love is perfected in us. The more His love is perfected in us, the less freedom fear has to control or consume us. "Perfect love casts out fear."

For each of us the fight against fear will be a battle we will fight until God's love ultimately is perfected in us when we enter the Pearly Gates. We always will battle with the monster in the closet. However, that monster does not have to consume us. Fear does not have to overwhelm us. In Christ, we can win!

One day, after struggling for years when I was alone at night with my kids, I realized that God had brought me to a place in which I felt safe. Four years after the initial robbery, my trust in Him was tested when my husband was invited to spend three weeks in Indonesia. I was to keep our two girls by myself at our home in northeast Brazil. I still had no relatives on the same continent. I still didn't even have friends I could call in a pinch. I still had no access to ambulances or emergency services. But, for the first time in a long time, I slept soundly at night in my own bedroom without fear.

The difference, and the only difference, was that in five years I had learned to trust in the Lord a little better. I had learned to give my children, as best as I could, to the Lord. I had learned that I could trust our physical safety in His hands. I had learned, at least for the moment, what the writer of Romans has been trying to tell us Christians for thousands of years: "In all these things we are more than conquerors through Him who loved us. For I am persuaded that neither death nor life, nor angels nor principalities nor powers, nor things present nor things to come, nor height nor depth, nor any other created thing, shall be able to separate us from the love of God which is in Christ Jesus our Lord" (Rom. 8:37-39).

We are in a spiritual war. Fear is the monster that lives in everyone's closets. He can live right next to our beds. During the course of our lives he will change clothes and pop up in different places, but He is the same dreadful and ever-powerful spiritual enemy. We have only one way to defeat Him: fight Him with the whole armor of God—truth, righteousness, preparation of the gospel of peace, faith, and the sword of the spirit, which is the Word of God. Learn to use the weapons God has given us. Fight him, slay him, and LIVE victoriously in power, in love, and in a sound mind.

Value 11

Making Authentic Friendships

Michael W. Smith was an icon on the American Christian-music scene in the '80s—the decade of my adolescence. I remember singing his music in church and purchasing his tapes. When I was in the ninth grade, our youth group went to Six Flags to see him in concert. My senior year in high school I even performed in *Friends are Friends Forever,* a musical he wrote.

The occasion was momentous. My mother put in our family scrapbook a picture of the closing song. The entire youth group was on the stage. My hair was permed, my collar was pulled up, and my pants legs were folded and tucked into my hot-pink socks. My best friend, Lari Bateman, was on one side of me. My good friend, Alan Ater, was on the other. Our arms were interlocked; the high-school choir was behind us. "And friends are friends forever, if the Lord's the Lord of them. And a friend will not say never . . ." the song went. We were singing our hearts out and meaning every word. This likely would be the last time we ever were to see each other. Our hearts were pounding to the beat of the slow-tempoed music.

Our youth group was not a typical youth group. We met for only two weeks a year: one week in January and the other in July. However, we were very close. We loved each other. We all were MK's, or missionary kids, living across the nation of Brazil. We had known each other for years and were bonded by similar life experiences. The people on the front row were those whose numbers had been called. The time had arrived for us to go "home" to the U.S. and leave our friends and families. Over the next few weeks we each would board a plane and head back to our homeland—a land we hardly knew. All of us had tears in our eyes. The night of the musical was our last night together. We stayed up all night playing Spades, dancing to Cindy Lauper, and making loud noises in our hotel. It was bittersweet. I never will forget it.

Friendship is an interesting phenomenon. Sociologists claim that from the time we start attending school, our friends play a more important role in shaping who we become than even our parents do. We value friends' opinions more than we do those of our family and sometimes even of God Himself. Our friends have a say on everything from what kind of underwear we wear to what careers are worth pursuing. We take great physical and emotional risks for our friends to love us and think highly of us. Yet, at the end of the night, as in my case, we sign each other's yearbooks, pass out addresses, pledge eternal love and loyalty, hug deeply, then walk out of each other's lives and into the next relationship: equally as vulnerable, equally as needy for affirmation and attention.

The truth of the matter is that most friends are not forever. In fact, generally they are temporary. For the most part the people that I love today are people that I have known for fewer than five years. We are friends because of the circumstances of our lives. We meet and, for some reason or another, we connect at some level and become friends. We live in the same place. We do the same kinds of things. We share the same space in the world. However, when they or I change spaces, we likely no longer will be close friends—not because we or they are bad people, but because our circumstances in life change. Most of my friends from high school, although I still have warm feelings for them, are not part of my core group of friends today. We have moved on; our lives have changed. Those things that made us friends 15 years ago are not as important anymore. Our connection is weak. So, in some sense, we all are nothing but a bunch of scavengers—always looking for the next friend to walk into our lives. This is natural; it's the human experience.

The Bible actually has interesting stories and something to say about friends and how to find the ones that will last a lifetime. Solomon made this very cynical, however true, observation that friends can be bought: "The poor man is hated even by his own neighbor, But the rich man has many friends" (Prov. 14:20).

Since the days of the old kings, friendship sometimes can mean nothing more than popularity. Popularity is a commodity. We hate to admit it, but even in church, it is for sale. It can be bought with cash, authority, good looks, or an interesting personality. Friendship, however, in this very shallow sense of the word, is nothing more than a powerful illusion. Jesus tells the story of the son who goes out into the world to seek his fortune. He lives with great gusto and enjoys life with lots of money, girls, booze, and whatever else was cool in the first century. However, eventually, the money runs out and with it, so do his friends. In shame he is forced to return home. The glamour is all a beautiful mirage; in the end he is alone.

But, even if we have good, quality people that befriend us, in general most friends will waltz into our lives and eventually will waltz out. Most friendships always will be superficial. In our lives we will not be remarkably close to very many people. Friendships—the kind that truly are meaningful—are difficult to find. They take work, sacrifice, and selflessness to build. But, if and when they do exist, they really can last forever.

These special, lifelong friends are the ones we can call collect after we declare bankruptcy. They are the ones who walk with us and hold our hands as we cry through a painful divorce or a humiliating professional crisis. They are the people who will tell the truth when doing so makes us want to hate them. They are the ones that make life special and make us want to be better people, because we know someone actually cares.

We long to connect deeply with someone and feel as though our worlds are bonded in a deep and spiritual way. We want friendships that are more real even than are our bonds of blood. But for the most part, this always will elude us. A large number, maybe even most people, actually live their entire lives and never have a single person they can call a real, lifelong friend. Why is this true? How can I avoid letting this happen to me?

"A man who has friends must himself be friendly, But there is a friend who sticks closer than a brother" (Prov. 18:24).

To be friendly means to be the kind of person that makes a good friend—be a person of good character who honors God deeply and has a high commitment to loyalty.

The best biblical example of friendship is that of David and Jonathan. The Bible does nothing to describe how these two met, what they had in common, how they hung out, or why they even were friends. We can imagine what initially drew them together. Jonathan was first in line to the throne. He was handsome, a mighty warrior, well-bred, and obviously an eligible bachelor. He more than likely was in a position to throw the best parties in town. David also was handsome (the Bible says he was), talented (a musician), athletic (killed Goliath), smart, and a lady's man. He probably was fun to hang out with and also was very popular. At first their fate and natures likely brought them together. David and Jonathan actually even were brothers-in-law. However, the same fate that brought them together might well could have torn them apart.

In 1 Samuel 20 David and Jonathan make a vow of loyalty that demonstrates how deeply they are bonded together. Still as young men, they swear to be loyal to each other forever, no matter what happens in the political world. The Bible says that "Jonathan again caused David to vow, because he loved him; for he loved him as he loved his own soul."

The next day Jonathan discovers that his father is on a mission to kill David as a threat to the throne. Jonathan risks his life to warn David and helps him escape the country. On the day David departs, the Bible says "they kissed one another; and they wept together, but David more so." Their hearts are broken because they are deeply bonded in their spirits. Their friendship is "closer than a brother."

But a friendship such as this only works if I am a person with upstanding character who honors God. God chose David and not Jonathan to be king. David is in the way of Jonathan's career—his fortune, his success, his dreams from childhood. Jonathan's interests directly conflict with David's fate. Jonathan is in a position to sell out David. He himself could kill David. But their friendship is worth more to Jonathan than is the entire nation of Israel. Jonathan has honorable character. He is selfless before God. He is loyal, even to the point of giving up his rightful place to the throne in preference to God's choice.

People like that are very rare. Most people do not have the character to be a friend to anyone besides themselves. We tend to be loyal first and foremost to ourselves. We say, "I will be your friend as long as my friendship with you serves my purposes. I will help you only if it doesn't conflict with my personal self-interest."

Jeff and I have been blessed to have in our lives friends that are men and women of character. Since we got married, probably the closest friends Jeff and I have are David and Laurie Bledsoe. We first met David and Laurie after we moved to Memphis after our stint in Japan. David was an engineer and Laurie a schoolteacher. David was one semester ahead of Jeff, but both were just beginning seminary and didn't know all that seminary life would entail. Neither of us had any children. Our lives originally were put together through life circumstances, but that is not what has made us friends.

During the last seven years David and Laurie's lives have been put under a microscope right before my very eyes. We struggled together as we believed God was leading us to a deeper involvement and bigger commitment to missions. David and Laurie applied and were accepted for appointment as career missionaries to the country of Brazil three months before we were. Under my observant eye they had their first child two years before we had our first. We were in language school together; we watched them adjust to a foreign culture. We watched them remodel their first house on the mission field, only to have the painter accidentally paint their entire house turquoise instead of beige! They could do nothing about it. We watched David accidentally miss the birth of their second child because he couldn't get through their city of three million people in time to be there. We watched them as their daughter struggled with bronchitis and asthma. We prayed with them as David was caught in the middle of a gang crossfire shooting. I have called Laurie collect in the middle of the night from the hospital when my child was sick. I have called her collect at other times for mundane things such as checking a phone number or doing a favor for my father. For the last seven years not much that has happened in the lives of David and Laurie Bledsoe did not get noticed by Jeff and Christy Brawner. My judgement, after seven years of observation, is that David and Laurie Bledsoe are two of the most godly people I know. They have demonstrated grace under fire and made the right decisions under pressure. Most remarkable to me, but perhaps not as important, is that they have done so while living a life filled with fun, humor, and excitement—at least most of the time.

The Bible says, "As iron sharpens iron, So a man sharpens the countenance of his friend" (Prov. 27:17). I want to be friends with people such as David and Laurie because they are people who are sharp and that can sharpen me: make me a better person, challenge me, and force me to be more than I think I can be. To have such a friend, I must aspire to be such a friend. Of course I do not claim to be all the things I have claimed David and Laurie to be (the truth be told, they probably don't claim them, either). However, I do claim to aspire to this: I am trying to be the kind of person who is worthy of a worthy friend.

Don't rush into a bunch of deep friendships. Choose your friends carefully and slowly. Make for your closest friends people with good character and who honor God deeply because, in the course of life, things will happen.

Time is necessary to really see people's character. Some people are good fakers. Once I had a work colleague whom I thought would be a friend. We lived overseas in the same city and in a very isolated situation. At the time we both worked for the same organization. We actually had a lot in common. Not long after I started working for the company, our team was invited to send a field representative to a conference in a neighboring country. It was a two-day, all-expenses-paid trip. I very much wanted to be the representative for our team. I still was going through some major culture-shock issues and wanted the break, not to mention a free trip! I talked individually to everyone on our team and discovered that no one really even liked being the representative. The trip agenda was really tight and left little free time to tour. Most of my colleagues really were too busy to be interested. That excited me all the more. I was the only one interested. It was a no-brainer. A meeting was scheduled; among other things we were to select our representative. I was ready to pack my bag. The day of the meeting finally arrived. The meeting was long; the vote was the very last item on the agenda. Five o'clock arrived; we still were meeting. Because the meeting ran long, I had to slip out of the meeting for a few minutes. My "friend", realizing her opportunity, seized the moment. In a few short moments she took the floor and explained all the reasons why I was underqualified to represent our team. She stated that she had more seniority than I did and was more deserving of this position. The woman was my friend. I would have expected her to be my advocate. She had told me she had no interest in the trip. The leader of our team also was shocked. He announced that we would take no vote. The selection of the representative was his prerogative; the vote merely was a courtesy. Since seniority was a criterion for team representation, the older member would be selected. The leader barely had voiced his decision before I waltzed back into the room. Oblivious to the lingering, awkward silence, I had been betrayed.

This woman hurt me—not because she had wanted to be the team representative, but because she was not loyal. Unfortunately, no matter how difficult this is for me to WRITE, she was deceitful. Her character was flawed. In fairness, we all are deceivers. Everyone has a history of telling things that are not true. However, deceit is a character trait that must be tamed by the almighty God. My youngest daughter once confessed to me that she had a tough time telling the truth. "I'll quit lying when I get to heaven," she confessed in utter despair.

For 3-year-old Elizabeth, to always tell the truth was as unattainable on this earth as were the Pearly Gates themselves. However, she was trying to work it out.

When we practice deceit, we ruin relationships. Of course this woman long since has left my life, but after that incident our relationship immediately changed. I did not believe she was a person worthy of my trust and loyalty. We were able to be colleagues and to see each other socially. We worked together and were cordial. I really had no bad feelings about the trip, but that day I learned that I could not afford to invest my heart into that relationship. She was not the kind of friend I wanted to have in my life.

We all have stories of betrayal. We all have stories of choosing bad friends. The reason we do is that most of us don't use the right criteria when we originally pick our friends. If I look back over the course of my life, I admit that at times I have had exceedingly shallow criteria in selecting the people to whom I chose to be close. When I make a list of all my past "best friends" and the people into whom I tried to invest my heart, I end up with a very diverse list of primarily women: a person who now is a lawyer, a government bureaucrat, a speech pathologist, a biologist, several business-women, a minister, a piano-bar singer, a teacher, a psychologist, a missionary, and several full-time moms. These women are as diverse as are their jobs.

As I looked at my list, I wondered what common characteristic they all shared. I didn't take more than a few seconds to evaluate my subconscious criteria for friend-picking: all my friends are drop-dead gorgeous. Did I set out to pick beautiful friends? I don't remember ever thinking such a thought, but could good looks possibly have been the top of my list of values?

Amazingly, only four of those today are even in my Microsoft Outlook list of contacts. My criterion was superficial. Being beautiful does not qualify anyone to be a good friend. It has nothing to do with any of the attributes that one needs to build a lasting bond. In fact, because I had such shallow criteria, only by God's grace did I not choose friends that actually could harm me or wrongly influence me. "As iron sharpens iron" could go the other way.

One young woman in the Bible understood friendship and devotion much better than I did at her age. God honored her by grafting her almost miraculously into Jesus' bloodline. Her story is recorded in the Bible. Her name carries the title and takes precedence over the author.

Ruth and Naomi were related by marriage and lived together in the land of Moab. For 10 years life was good. They were natural allies. Their lives were going in the same direction. But circum-stances changed. Things became difficult. Both of their husbands died. They became poor. They were women with no legal or ethical means of supporting themselves. Naomi, the mother-in-law, loved Ruth and recognized that Ruth had no choice but to return to her father and to try to find another husband. She, in turn, would return to her homeland and try to live subsistently off the mercies of gen-erous, old relatives who hopefully had not forgotten her during her long absence. She had a dismal future and one that most assuredly guaranteed an early death.

Ruth listened to Naomi's explanation and realized she could not abandon her dear friend to the chances of fate. No matter if doing so cost her her life, Ruth would be faithful and would try to save the life of her dear friend, Naomi. In so many words she told Naomi that she was going with her, whether or not Naomi wanted her to do so. In the biblical account Ruth gave the most eloquent rebuttal and expression of friendship recorded in the Bible:

"Entreat me not to leave you, Or to turn back from following after you; For wherever you go, I will go; And wherever you lodge, I will lodge; Your people shall be my people, And your God my God. Where you die, I will die, And there I will be buried. The LORD do so to me, and more also, If anything but death parts you and me" (Ruth 1:16-17).

This is the nature of true, lifelong friendship. Jesus says, "There is no greater love than this than a man to lay down his life for his friend." Although friends, just like romance, cannot take the place of God, true, lifelong friendships are among God's greatest gifts to us. They are holy and spring from the heart of God. They are rare but still real for those who invest in their own character and become worthy of the sacrifice.

Value 12

Knowing Thyself: An Heir by Grace

Remind them to be subject to rulers and authorities, to obey, to be ready for every good work, to speak evil of no one, to be peaceable, gentle, showing humility to all men. For we ourselves were also once foolish, disobedient, deceived, serving various lusts and pleasures, living in malice and envy, hateful and hating one another. But when the kindness and the love of God our Savior toward man appeared, not by works of righteousness which we have done, but according to His mercy He saved us, through the washing of regeneration and renewing of the Holy Spirit, whom He poured out on us abundantly through Jesus Christ our Savior, that having been justified by His grace, we should become heirs according to the hope of eternal life (Titus 3:1-6).

Most Americans, of which I am no exception, are enamored with all things British—from Wimbledon to Spice Girls to Shakespeare to Simon Cromwell. Yet perhaps the most fascinating aspect of modern England continues to be the monarchy. The modern-day queen has a unique role. This role creates a mysterious aura around a celebrated throne. How must one feel to be qualified to ride in a golden carriage, wear a crown with more than 3,000 precious gems, and live in the largest occupied castle in the world? What does being a prince of England mean?

As outsiders we have a tough time really understanding the patriotism and deep feelings on both sides of Windsor's walls. The king—the role, not the person *per se*—in part at least symbolizes what being British means. He is a source of pride, an authority, and a glory that is expressed in all the pomp and ceremony that surrounds the throne. He or she, whichever the case may be, is a living symbol of nationalism, a connection with history, and a reminder of a remarkable past.

Could anything be more glamorous than to be born into unimaginable wealth, immediate fame, immeasurable influence, and a secured place in history? Prince William and Prince Harry appear to be the luckiest people on earth. They embody what being beautiful, important, desirable—to be the envy of the world—means.

My daughter had an eyelash fall on her cheek. As part of a little family game we play, my other daughter, Anna, who saw the eyelash, picked it off her cheek and said, "Make a wish." Lizzy closed her eyes; I could tell she was wishing deeply. When she opened her eyes, I asked her, "What did you wish for?" Of course the rule is that you're not supposed to tell your wish, but Lizzy couldn't keep her secret, so she whispered in my ear, "I wished to be a princess."

To become a princess is the unfulfilled dream of almost every girl who ever saw a tiara. Sadly it is a dream that always will be unfulfilled. No one can become a princess: it is a birthright, not something earned by merit or purchase. Aspiring to be the queen of anything is a childhood fantasy. Kingdoms are passed along through the bloodline; no one ever can do anything about that.

Jesus Christ made a claim that was more audacious than any claim ever made on earth. This claim was so outrageous, his critics sarcastically nailed it over His head on the cross when they hung Him up to die. The sign read "King of the Jews." It was the biggest joke going on that dark day. But the sign-maker really didn't quite get it right. Jesus did not claim to be just King of the Jews. Jesus claimed to be King of Kings and Lord of Lords. He claimed to be King of the entire world: Jews, Greeks, Asians, Indians, Americans, Europeans, Africans—everyone! He claimed to be worthy of ALL power, ALL honor, ALL strength, ALL wisdom, and ALL riches ever to exist or have ever existed—not just on earth but in the entire universe. He claimed to be over everything, not just "in this age but also in the one to come" (Eph. 1:21). He claimed this and then sought to prove His right to the throne by defeating humankind's greatest enemy—the one no earthly king or warrior, no matter how powerful, ever has been able to defeat: DEATH itself.

After allowing Himself to be nailed on the cross, Jesus lay dead for three days and then arose from the grave, the Bible says. He defeated death and proved that He was who He said He is—the Creator and rightful ruler of the universe—far above any principality, power, dominion, or might.

This is the most amazing story ever to cross the history books of humankind, but it doesn't end with Jesus' ascending into heaven. In Titus 3:5-6, the Bible reteaches one more very important concept that Jesus spent His entire ministry trying to beat into our stubborn heads: "But when the kindness and the love of God our Savior toward man appeared, not by works of righteousness which we have done, but according to His mercy He saved us, through the washing of regeneration and renewing of the Holy Spirit, whom He poured out on us abundantly through Jesus Christ our Savior, that having been justified by His grace, we should become heirs according to the hope of eternal life."

We have been chosen to become HEIRS in Christ's kingdom—the ultimate kingdom, with all the benefits of sonship. The day we accept Christ into our hearts, the Bible teaches us that by GRACE, meaning not by anything we have done to deserve it, but for free, He has adopted us into the royal family. We are entitled to all the benefits of such a legacy.

We are significant and important in life, not because of our intelligence, our beauty, or our place of birth here on this earth, but because of our place of birth into the family of God. In that sense being a member of God's family is similar to being a member of the British royal family. If we look at the history of England, we see that the right to the throne never had anything to do with virtue of position. Instead it had everything to do with DNA and the bloodline.

Elizabeth Tudor was the apparently insignificant younger daughter of King Henry VIII. She was third in line to the throne behind her half-brother, Edward, and her sister, Mary. Her brother became King Edward, but he died early of consumption. Her half-sister, Mary, then became the Bloody Queen Mary. She turned out to be a horrible woman who murdered thousands and even locked up her baby sister, Elizabeth, in the Tower of London—the place in which Elizabeth's own mother had been beheaded by their father, Henry VIII. Elizabeth seemed unlikely to do anything significant.

As history would play itself out, this would not be the case. Elizabeth became the most celebrated ruler in her family. In fact her reign as the Queen of England is referred to as the "Golden Age." She led England to live in peace and became a prosperous world player.

How did Elizabeth become queen? Beauty? Wit? Personal merit? A successful job-application process? Of course none of those things applied. She was the rightful heir to the throne. This tradition was so powerful that countries throughout history have done what the English did: they put someone on the throne, not because of her education, preparation, a job interview, or political merit. She was queen solely because of her blood. It was the only requirement; she was the only one in all of England who was qualified to fulfill it.

Christ says we are heirs to the throne. The reason we are heirs is exactly the same: our blood—but then again, it's not our blood; it's the blood of Jesus Christ splashed across our hearts and souls that defines who we are from the moment we pray and ask Him into our lives. Just as in the case of Elizabeth Tudor, the bloodline will be the difference between life and death. We are, in a manner of speaking, princes and princesses of the Most High God. Everyone reborn in His blood has value and significance because of a personal relationship and a blood connection with King Jesus. I, Christy Akins Brawner, am a princess by God's grace—an heiress to the King of Kings!

A major difference exists, however, between our heritage and that of the Virgin Queen—none of us ever will rule. Jesus Christ is the immortal King. No Heavenly Queen ever will be. From the Virgin Mary down to the criminal on the cross, we all are subject to the King of Kings. The throne is secure; Christ Eternal will reign forever.

Since before the beginning of history Satan has tried to overthrow the throne of God. He was not content to be a servant of the Most High. He coveted the throne. The Bible calls him the prince of this world because he was banished from heaven and, with his legion of fallen angels, roams among us. When Christ defeated death on the cross, He defeated Satan once and for all.

However Satan still continues to be the prince of the world. He is the prince of the power of the air. He will roam freely until Christ returns to take His rightful place and to throw Satan in the infamous fiery pit God himself has prepared for him. Satan's sole mission in life is to destroy as much of humanity as possible before Christ's return. His mission on earth is to destroy every one of us. He wants to fill us with hate, envy, self-loathing, underconfidence, guilt, depression, and ultimately, death. He goes after us one by one. He identifies our weaknesses and lies in our ears.

We do not have to fall prey to his deceit. "The Spirit Himself bears witness with our spirit that we are children of God, and if children, then heirs—heirs of God and joint heirs with Christ, if indeed we suffer with Him, that we may also be glorified together" (Rom. 8:16-17).

During some times in our lives, we will goof up. We will have times of immense regret or remorse and will wish they had not happened. But nothing can be done to replay the past. It's over; all we have left are the bitter consequences of our actions.

It is part of our humanity. All of us do this—even those of the purest blood. Yet, the Bible teaches that nothing that we ever could do has the power to define who we are. No act can change our place in God's heart and in His love and purpose for us. He accepted us freely. Ephesians 2:4 says, "But God, who is rich in mercy, because of His great love with which He loved us, even when we were dead in trespasses, made us alive together with Christ (by grace you have been saved)" Learn to live a life that is full of grace. We are forgiven and entitled to live by grace. It is our place; it is our legacy; it is our calling. But what does grace mean?

The Portuguese word for grace is *graça*. I never heard the word *grace* used very much outside of church until we moved to Brazil. In Portuguese I started to hear the word used almost every day. The reason Brazilians use this word every day is not because they are extremely religious but because it is their word for "free", meaning something costs nothing. It is undeserved. We took our daughters to the mall to visit a June Festival exhibit. In the middle of the exhibit were tables set up for children, with monitors, to color and do art projects. I told the girls they couldn't go until the woman in charge turned to me and said *de graça*, meaning "by grace"—the exhibit was free. We are heirs *de graça*. It changes our perspective on things. In the case of the art projects, we participated.

Have grace on yourself. Quit punishing yourself for trying to make yourself pay penance for things you have done in your past. "If we confess our sins, he is faithful and just to forgive us our sins, and to cleanse us from all unrighteousness" (1 John 1:9). Once we ask God to forgive us of something, as far as He's concerned, it's over. It does not hang over our heads. It does not reflect who we are or what we are worth.

The Bible says that when we sin, God convicts us and makes us feel badly about what we have done. "Your sorrow led to repentance. For you were made sorry in a godly manner." He wants us to recognize our errors in order for us to change but not for condemnation. A huge difference lies between the two.

When I was in the 10th grade, an older friend invited me to go with her on a train to visit relatives in the interior of Brazil. I was excited about going. The interior of Brazil can be very primitive. People still ride around on horses; a milk man actually rides by every morning with fresh milk from the cow. We were going "back in time" without our parents. It was exciting. My best friend, Becky, also was invited. Only one problem existed: no adult chaperones were around. My friend had a brother my age who I had been casually dating. My mother, who was no dummy, made a firm rule. I still remember her words ringing in my head, "You can go if no boys are going. Can you give me that assurance?" "Of course, Mom; Becky's mom never would allow that," I lied. Becky's mom was in the dark as much as my mother was.

I never had lied to my mother. As soon as the words emerged from my mouth, I could feel the weight of guilt on me. It was awful. Day and night all I could think about was the horrible deception. We went on the trip, but the trip was tainted. I was miserable. In fact Becky didn't have any fun either. The trip was a total bust: a waste of money, a waste of time, and a waste of energy. All we wanted to do was get home. After two days we decided to leave.

But leaving the interior proved to be impossible. No buses went out of that little town. The train just didn't stop by whenever we wanted it to. We were stuck.

Finally we left and returned home. Once again I had to face my mother. I was so ashamed. I didn't know what to say, so I did the most convenient thing: continued the lie. Mother, who had complete faith in me, never asked; I never volunteered any information. Life just went back to normal. The problem was that the truth nagged me day and night. This went on for days, then weeks, and then months. I couldn't quit thinking about this deception. I remember arguing with God, "Leave me alone. It's not like I hurt anybody or did anything wrong. Don't other people do worse things? Just let me forget about it. Let me go to sleep." But the Holy Spirit never did until one day, months and months after the trip, I sat at my desk and penned a letter telling my mother everything. I was so embarrassed at what I had done. I was a liar. I didn't even have the nerve to face her. I left the letter under her pillow for her to find when she went to sleep.

That night, unable to sleep, I lay in my bed. I waited for my mother to find my letter. Finally I heard her walk down the hallway and knock on my door. When she opened the door, I began to sob uncontrollably as the Holy Spirit finally freed me from my guilt. "Godly sorrow produces repentance," says 2 Corinthians 7:10. Of course my mother forgave me. She didn't even punish me. The deception in my heart was much worse than was any overt offense I had committed. I felt an overwhelming sense of relief. It was over.

"The sorrow of the world produces death." Another kind of guilt exists: false guilt. Satan makes us feel guilty for things that God already has forgiven. He puts ghosts in our closets and brings them out at night to tell us how horrible we are and that our lives have no redeeming value. False guilt is condemning. It doesn't seek restoration. It seeks our destruction. I knew a young man who was bright, funny, good-looking, and the joy of his parents' lives. He was a good son, a model citizen, and was accepted into a well-reputed university. After he got into college, however, he began mingling with a gothic crowd. He began listening to sad music, wearing black, and flirting with the darker side of life. He quit attending our church and was doing his own thing. We had not heard from him for several years. One day we received a fateful phone call. This young man had been found in his grandfather's field with a bullet hole in his head. It was a total shock. No one could understand what could have driven this man to such utter hopelessness and despair. What had caused this depression and stolen away the hope and life of such a beautiful person? Later, his secret emerged. He had been sleeping with a girl who was not his fiancé. This girl, in an attempt to blackmail him into leaving his fiancé, told him she was carrying his child. In a letter he confessed his guilt. He felt guilt about the relationship. He felt badly for his fiancé. He felt trapped and isolated in his situation. He felt overwhelmed. He felt shame and despair. He felt hopelessness. He felt condemned. His guilt was not from God.

As an outsider looking at this situation, one easily can say to the young man: "You created a problem, but you have a solution." For those that are emotionally uninvolved in the situation, seeing how God could fix all of this is not difficult. But, through the eyes of this young man, all he could see was darkness and shame. He was blinded by guilt, but this was not guilt. It was false guilt. God forgives. God restores. God gives hope. "If we confess our sins, He is faithful and just to forgive us our sins, and to cleanse us from all unrighteousness" (1 John 1:9). How sad that this young man did not know the difference!

A grave difference exists between the two. We cannot put away the conviction of the Holy Spirit; it is honest and true. It leads us to repentance—to change our ways and live a life that is better than the one we are living. Jesus told the woman caught in adultery, "Neither do I condemn you. Arise and sin no more."

False guilt is from the devil. It can and must be overcome. "The sorrow of the world produces death" (2 Cor. 7:10).

Satan wants to throw our errors and embarrassments in our faces. He wants to taunt us. He wants to devalue us. He wants us to remember over and over and over again, until our torment leads us to the point of death. This is Satan's goal for all of our lives—utter destruction. He can do this if he can make us forget that we are heirs—not by merit but by grace. God does not hold me in contempt for those things that His Son's blood has covered. So, if God is not judging me, how do I become free from this torment?

Doing this is not easy, but it is possible. First, confess your sin. Admit that you have sinned before God. If you have sinned against someone else, then you face the uncomfortable experience of going privately to the people you have offended and asking forgiveness. Notice the importance of the word "privately." You have no need (in fact, doing so actually is harmful) to "air dirty laundry in the front yard." You can live a life free from hypocrisy and still keep past things in the past.

Secondly, claim your place of freedom in Jesus' name and refuse to entertain thoughts of condemnation. Every time a condemning thought enters your mind for something Christ already has forgiven, stop, quote 1 John 1:9, and say in your head, "I refuse to feel guilty for this. I am forgiven. I am free." If you will do this over and over and over, finally, one day, the enemy will stop nagging you about the incident. Satan even quit pestering Jesus in the desert after Jesus answered him three times and used the Bible as a weapon. He may start picking on us in some other areas of our lives. However, even the enemy doesn't haunt us about the same things if we continue to recall Scripture about the problem.

Live a life free from shame—a life free from dark secrets. I am innocent because I am forgiven, not because I am perfect. I don't have to pretend to merit a place seated on top of anyone's footstool. But I do stand tall next to anyone in the room knowing I am just as worthy, just as important, just as precious to the King as that person is. Live a life of GRACE. I am an heiress by grace, not merit.

You can find a flipside to being an heir of grace. This is reflected in the passage of Scripture at the top of the chapter. Because we are heirs, we can afford and are fully expected by King Jesus himself to treat others with the kind of grace that has been shown to us.

Every night, after my girls wash their hair, they each take turns and sit on my lap for me to comb through the tangles. On days they have not used conditioner, doing this is a true nightmare. The process can require more than 30 minutes. Our neighbors can hear us over two nine-foot walls of separation. From my daughters' perspective they submit to someone deliberately causing them pain and discomfort. I still remember the early days when I started this ritual with Anna, my oldest daughter. Every night she would go away angry. I didn't know what to do about it until one day I had a stroke of genius. I told her, "Anna, if I hurt you, just hit me back as hard as I hurt you. If I pulled your hair hard, hit me on my leg hard. If I pulled your hair softly, hit me on my leg softly." She agreed to this deal. Every time I pulled her hair, she hit me. By the end of the combing she was not angry. Her anger had been vented; she felt vindicated.

This is fascinating. Somehow, we have an inner need for revenge. If someone cuts me off in traffic, I feel better if I honk at that person, although admittedly, nothing changes. Part of the human condition is at least to wish harm on those that deserve it, even when we are powerless to impose it. But this is not the posture of someone who is an heir to the throne.

Titus tells his readers to "be subject to rulers and authorities, to obey", though in his day, they all were corrupt and evil. He says to be ready for every good work. He says to "speak evil of no one", even though most all the authorities likely deserve whatever verbal damage you could inflict. He says to be peaceable, to be gentle, and to show all humility to all men.

Then he gives a reason. He says to do this because you are an heir of grace. You have nothing to prove. "Vengeance is mine, I will repay, says, the Lord." I, as an heir, do not have to defend myself. I do not have to make things right. I can live in the absolute freedom that God will take care of me.

Every year for Christmas, my grandmother had a tradition of giving me a Madame Alexander® doll. To this day, I cherish these dolls. When my daughter, Anna Katherine, turned 1, my grandmother sent her a Madame Alexander® baby doll. It was not like the dolls that stand up in cupboards; this was a doll with which she could play. That was exactly what Anna Katherine did with her doll. She immediately ripped it out of the box and fell in love with it. She named the baby "Baby Landon", even though the baby was a girl. She carried Baby Landon everywhere. When we moved from

São Paulo to Fortaleza, Baby Landon was in a seat on the plane. When we arrived, she toted that baby to every church in the city, to every grocery store, to every home she visited. Baby Landon was a part of the family until one day something sad happened. We had spent the day at a very, very poor church on the outskirts of our town. All day Jeff and I team-taught a seminar. We had brought a babysitter to help us watch the girls. They had brought toys and coloring books to keep them entertained for the day. Because this was a poor neighborhood, when Anna and Elizabeth showed up at the church with toys, all the kids with any connection to the church turned out to play in the "nursery" (a patio behind the church). The girls loved this and played all day. At five o'clock we finished the seminar and loaded the car with the toys to return home. Everyone was in the car when Anna, in her broken baby-talk, said "Wheer Baby Landon?" We got out and looked. We called the pastor over to see if he knew. Baby Landon was gone. Baby Landon had walked off in the arms of one of the other little girls. For the trip home Anna was inconsolable. She didn't understand why someone would take her baby. It was *her* baby. I understood her pain and tried to explain it to her this way, "Anna, please don't be sad. You have lots and lots of dolls. In fact, Momma can get you another baby just like her. Baby Landon is going to be with a little girl who doesn't have a baby at all."

This didn't mean much to Anna, but it was true. Anna has been born to privilege. She is an American. She is very rich in comparison to most of the kids around her. She lives with both her parents who love her and give her just about anything in the world she ever could want or need. For a 2-year-old to lose a doll that has become a friend is devastating. However, from an adult perspective, it's OK. I knew that in the long run, Anna was going to be OK. We could cover that loss. We didn't want her to spend her time being angry at a little girl who has nothing. We wanted her to forgive the child, seek her well-being, and treat her with kindness the next time we see the child. Anna's daddy was going to make it all right. After all, much awaited her in life that will exceed the joy she received from Baby Landon.

Although this may be a simple analogy, this is the way God desires for us to live our lives: full of grace. This means granting forgiveness when someone yells at us or treats us improperly; refusing to harbor bitterness or anger when we may very well have the right to do so, or acting arrogant when we don't receive the respect we rightfully deserve.

The heir to the throne of England has nothing to prove. He is the heir. He can afford to show grace and mercy. No one challenges his rightful position. In the same way, live your life filled with grace: refusing malice, envy, foolishness, and hate. God purchased us with His blood; He made us heirs of grace to live a life of freedom and joy. He has a lifetime of joy prepared for us. If that weren't enough, one day when this life is over, we have eternity—one He has prepared for us. We don't have time or energy to spend in anger, resentment, or foolish pride. Our Father has taken care of everything and desires for us the best life can offer: a life lived in the fullness of Him—life lived gracefully and in freedom.

God bless you. Every day of your life may you seek to know God more deeply. May you find true spirituality in a personal relationship with your Creator and Redeemer. May you live a life of freedom, love, victory, and grace!

The Brawner family: Christy and Jeff, with Elizabeth (left) and Anna Katherine.

Order more copies of

How to Be Spiritual without Being Weird

Call toll free: 1-800-747-0738

Visit: *www.hannibalbooks.com*
Email: *hannibalbooks@earthlink.net*
FAX: 1-888-252-3022
Mail copy of form below to:
Hannibal Books
P.O. Box 461592
Garland, Texas 75046

Number of copies desired _____
Multiply number of copies by $9.95 _____

Please add $3 for postage and handling for first book and add
50 cents for each additional book in the order.
Shipping and handling$_____
Texas residents add 8.25% sales tax $_____

Total order $_____

Mark method of payment:
check enclosed _____
Credit card# _____
exp. date____ (Visa, MasterCard, Discover, American Express accepted)

Name _____

Address _____

City State, Zip _____

Phone _____ FAX _____

Email _____

You'll enjoy these missions books also

Be a 24/7 Christian by Wade Akins. Want to make Jesus truly the Lord your life but don't know how? This renowned missionary evangelist/strategist and father of Christy Brawner tells how to live the adventure of being totally sold out to the Lord every moment of every day, every day of every year.

_____Copies at $9.95=_____

Rescue by Jean Phillips. American missionaries Jean Phillips and her husband, Gene, lived through some of the most harrowing moments in African history of the last half century. Abducted and threatened with death, Jean and Gene draw on God's lessons of a lifetime.

_____Copies at $12.95=_____

Servant on the Edge of History by Sam James. What led American Sam James to allow himself and his family to be in harm's way again and again in war-traumatized Vietnam? Read this untold story of the Vietnam Era, when members of the James family constantly risked their lives for the gospel in order to help their beloved Vietnamese people.

_____Copies at $12.95=_____

Beyond Surrender by Barbara J. Singerman. A dramatic story of one family's quest to bring light to a dark and desperate world. The Singermans serve in Benin, West Africa. When they surrender to missions, they confront spiritual warfare beyond anything they expect.

_____Copies at $12.95=_____

Add $3.00 shipping for first book, plus 50 cents for each additional book.
Shipping & handling _____
Texas residents add 8.25% sales tax _____
TOTAL ENCLOSED_____

check ____ or credit card # _____ exp. date_____
(Visa, MasterCard, Discover, American Express accepted)

Name _____

Address _____ Phone _____

City _____ State _____ Zip _____

For postal address, phone number, fax number, email address and other ways to order from Hannibal Books, see page 159.

Printed in the United States
44315LVS00002B/211-636